Camp Verde

Camp Verde

Texas Frontier Defense

Joseph Luther

Published by The History Press
Charleston, SC 29403
www.historypress.net

Cover image: Frederic Remington, *Bringing the Bugle to Bear*. Published in *Harper's Weekly*, 1887.

First published 2012
Second printing 2012

Manufactured in the United States

ISBN 978.1.60949.386.8

Library of Congress Cataloging-in-Publication Data

Luther, Joseph Neal, 1943-
Camp Verde : Texas frontier defense / Joseph Luther.
p. cm.
Includes bibliographical references and index.
ISBN 978-1-60949-386-8
1. Camp Verde (Tex. : Fort) 2. Kerr County (Tex.)--History, Military--19th century. 3. Indians of North America--Texas--History. I. Title.
F392.K35L88 2012
355.709764'884--dc23
2011050624

This book is dedicated to my devoted wife, Vicki Braglio Luther,
without whom nothing would be possible.

Contents

Acknowledgements 9
Introduction 11

1. Prehistoric Verde Valley 17
2. First Contact 22
3. Spanish Texas 27
4. The Lipan Apaches 39
5. The Penateka Comanches 47
6. Estados Unidos Mexicanos 60
7. Republic of Texas 65
8. Texas Rangers 71
9. The U.S. Army in Texas 81
10. Camp Davant 90
11. The Second United States Cavalry 94
12. Camels 107
13. The Surrender of Camp Verde, 1861 112
14. Camp Verde, CSA 117
15. Prison Canyon 126
16. Frontier Regiment and Organization 130
17. Camp Verde, USA, Reactivated 134
18. The Texas Militia 143
19. The Frontier Battalion 146

Conclusion	149
Notes	155
Selected Bibliography	181
Index	183
About the Author	191

Acknowledgements

My sincere appreciation for their kind consideration and cooperation is given to the following individuals, who provided inspiration, information, critique and support for this research: Donna Snow Robinson, my local editor; Becky LeJeune, acquisitions editor, The History Press; Clifford Caldwell, my good friend and Texana historian; Deb Johnson, photographer; Steve Stoutamire, Hill Country Archeological Association; Bryant Saner, Hill Country Archeological Association; Kay and Woody Woodward, Hill Country Archeological Association; Douglas Scott, historical archaeologist; Tom Hester, archaeologist; Al McGraw, TxDOT archaeologist; Clark Wernecke, Gault School of Archaeological Research; Feather Wilson, geohydrologist; Clarabelle Snodgrass, historian; Kathleen S. Walker, Schreiner University; Joe Herring, historian; Don Wilson, historian; Gerald Witt, historian; Johnny Wauqua, chairman of the Comanche Nation; Haskell Fine, historian; Joe Davis, Former Texas Ranger Foundation; Arthur Schmidt, Prison Canyon Ranch; Tibaut Bowman, Camp Verde Ranch; Sherrell H. Eckstein; Joe Armistead; Charles Domingues, land surveyor; Robert Newman, Central Appraisal District; Mike Coward, TxDOT; and Felipe Jimenez, Camp Verde Store.

Introduction

The history of the Verde Valley has been determined, in large measure, by the character of its environment. Historically, this geographic area has been dominated by a rugged karst[1] landscape of hills, valleys, streams, springs and lush river bottoms. Kerr County lies on the southeastern edge of the thirty-eight-thousand-square-mile Edwards Plateau.[2] Camp Verde is located on the banks of Verde Creek, in Kerr County, Texas. Although Kerr County did not officially organize until 1856, people have lived here for more than twelve thousand years. The canyonland environment was well suited to the needs of aboriginal peoples, providing water, wild game, edible plants, rock shelters and respite from cold winds and intense sunshine.

This region was once a vast, shallow inland sea that spread from the Gulf of Mexico to the Arctic Circle. This Cretaceous sea deposited the limestone that now caps the Edwards Plateau. About seventy million years ago, the sea drained from here, set in motion by the slow uplift of this part of the continent. This "Central Texas Uplift" began as the continental interior rose and the last Cretaceous sea was displaced.[3] Of note is the fact that thousands of feet of overlying, younger sediments have been stripped off this cap rock by erosion.

The Edwards group of geological formations covers most of Kerr County. The rest of the county is covered either by stream deposits all over the Guadalupe Watershed or the upper Glen Rose marls and thin-bedded limestone. Rivers and streams smoothed off the surface of the flat-lying limestone layers. The easily eroded limestone enabled these watercourses

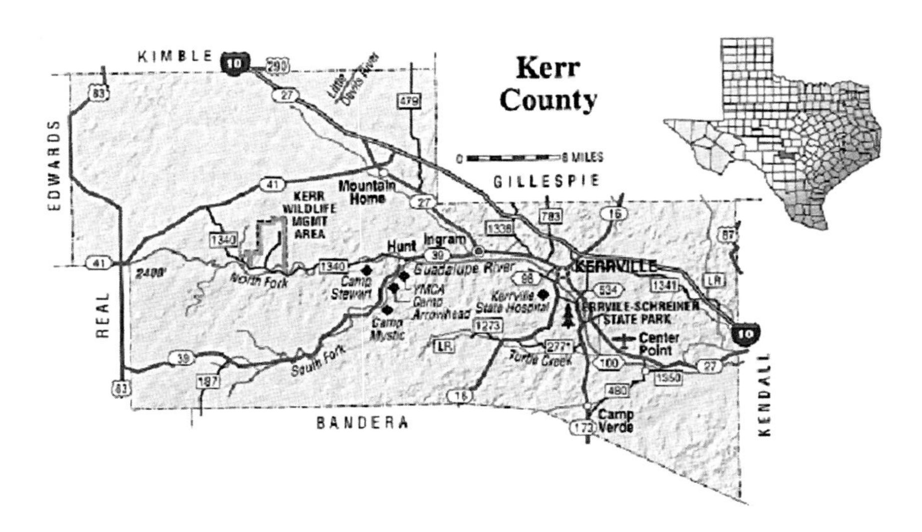

Map of Kerr County. *Used by permission of the Texas Almanac, www.TexasAlmanac.com.*

to establish themselves as river meanders, creating the scenic steep-walled valleys renowned today as the Hill Country. Most people think that the Hill Country consists of mountains, but in fact it consists of canyons and outliers left over from the capricious wanderings of stream courses as they etched their way in, around and through the Cretaceous sediments.

The famous Edwards Plateau is bounded by the Balcones Escarpment to the south and east, the Llano Uplift and the Llano Estacado to the north and the Pecos River and Chihuahuan Desert to the west. The Balcones Fault Zone was most recently active about fifteen million years ago during the Miocene epoch. This activity was related to subsidence of the Texas Coastal Plain, most likely from the large amount of sediment deposited on it by Texas rivers. The Balcones Fault Zone is not active today and is in one of the lowest-risk zones for earthquakes in the United States. The surface expression of the fault is the Balcones Escarpment, which forms the eastern boundary of the Texas Hill Country and the western boundary of the Texas Coastal Plain and consists of hills and cliff-like structures.[4]

The Guadalupe River is the major river traversing Kerr County. A number of creeks flow into the Guadalupe. The Verde Valley is an ancient coulee known for its natural beauty. The clear water of Verde Creek flows over limestone rocks as it runs from west to east, a distance of fourteen miles to a confluence with the Guadalupe River at the village of Center Point. The scenic cypress-lined waterway and lush grass valley provided the habitat for a wide range of wildlife over the centuries. These natural attributes attracted human settlement over a period of more than twelve thousand years.

The Spanish called the mountains on the south side of the Verde Valley the Guadalupe Mountains and Lomeria Grande (Big Hills).[5] This was the watershed divide between the Guadalupe River Basin and the Medina River Basin. The unique aspect of this particular valley that led to a geographical focus on the area was the existence of a mountain pass that provided a route from the southern coastal plains of Texas to the Edwards Plateau, the Llano Estacado and the west beyond. Known as Puerta de Bandera (Bandera Pass), this passage was one of only three easy routes to the west, the other two being Spanish Pass, known as Puerta de los Payayas, three miles north of Boerne, and the Arroyo de la Soledad (Sabinal River), known as Cañon de Ugalde, near today's Utopia.[6]

Camp Verde was the frontier. While other frontiers inexorably crept westward at a rate of ten miles a year, the frontier at Verde Valley remained

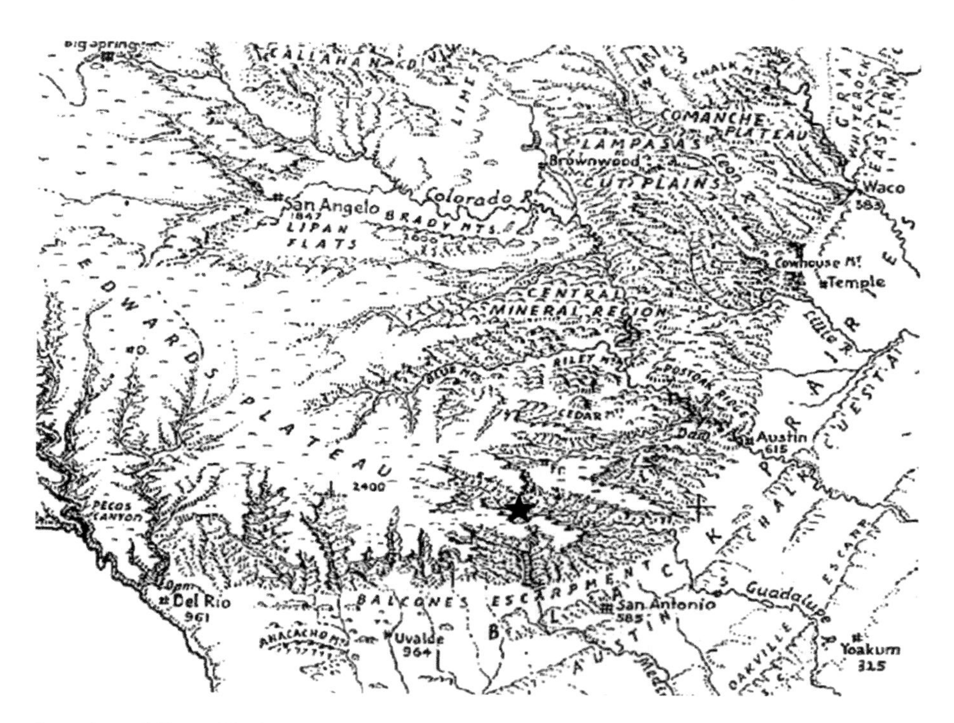

Location of Camp Verde. *Adapted with permission from* Physiographic Map of the United States, *drawn by Erwin Raisz, 1957.*

constant and unmoving. The reason was that Puerta de Bandera was a choke point of movement west. Beyond the frontier was the land of peril, adventure and mythic heroes. It was a wild and virgin environment of forests, mountains, caves, monsters and savages, at once a place of great beauty and unimaginable terror.

Tradition has it—and there is some evidence of truth to sustain the tale—that prior to 1732 the Indians made a treaty with the Spaniards by the terms of which the former agreed to forgo raids south of Bandera Pass and the Spaniards agreed not to encroach on the hunting grounds beyond that dividing range. Flags may have been planted on mountain peaks to mark this line. According to an eyewitness account dating to 1721, the Apaches stuck arrow shafts in the ground as an explicit warning. These arrows had red pieces of cloth attached to them like small flags.[7] These small flags (banderas) "signified a declaration of war."[8] While the source of the name "Puerta de Bandera" has been a mystery over the years, it seems most likely that the origin of the name was associated with this Apache war flag tradition.

Within a mile of Camp Verde is a hill given the Spanish name Monte del Mesa (29°53.198'N, 99°7.204'W).[9] Today, this hill is named Cedar Ridge and overlooks the site of the old Camp Verde army post. Local folklore tells a story that there is a stone table on top of this hill marking the place where Apaches signed a peace treaty with the Spanish soldiers. This may have been the peace treaty signed prior to 1732.

For sojourners passing through the rugged Puerta de Bandera, the frontier panorama did not yield its visage until the last moment. The trek was a gradual climb to the summit of the pass, screening the prospect until the last possible moment. What anticipation and anxiety this last mile must have created! From this vantage point, the vast frontier was remarkable. Travelers crossing to the north first caught sight of the rugged Hill Country. Those trekking south first glimpsed the Bandera Valley, the Balcones Escarpment and the coastal plain beyond.

The perception of the Texas frontier at Verde Valley is consistent with the setting popularized in literature such as James Fenimore Cooper's Leatherstocking Tales, including *The Last of the Mohicans*. The adventurer's imagination, stirred by visions of Nathaniel "Natty" Bumppo—known as Hawkeye—acted as a catalyst for crossing over the frontier into the savage wilderness.[10] Beyond Verde Valley lurked the frontier. Lucy Lockwood Hazard, in *The Frontier in American Literature* (1927), wrote, "The frontier affords the setting; it occasions the plot; it offers the theme; it creates the character."[11]

Bandera Pass, 1915. *Photo by Bryden Starr.*

"The novels of Cooper are an exercise in national definition," Marius Bewley wrote.[12] In *The Last of the Mohicans*, the national phase defined was the frontier. The concept of the frontier was a major theme composed, like the plot, of significant constituent parts. It was a place and a condition where differences met head-on and often resulted in conflict. According to Thomas Roundtree, "Since conflict is a basic ingredient of the frontier in the novel, the story's action of flight, skirmishing, disguise, warfare, etc. literally becomes theme."[13]

A frontier has two sides. For the Spanish, French and Euro-Americans, the frontier—with all its constituent elements—lay to the northwest. For the indigenous population of Native Americans, the frontier lay to the southeast. For each culture, there were significant elements of savagery and civilization, depending on one's frame of reference. As George Bernard Shaw noted, "The frontier between hell and heaven is only the difference between two ways of looking at things."[14] Each culture thought the other to be barbarous and itself to be civilized. The frontier at Verde Valley was not only a geopolitical setting but also the interface of very divergent cultures.

As the travelers trekked north or south through Puerta de Bandera, they changed. This is what Frederick Jackson Turner called "the significance of the frontier." Turner's "Frontier Thesis" was presented in a scholarly paper in 1893. He believed the spirit and success of the United States was directly tied to the country's westward expansion.[15] The forging of the unique and rugged American identity occurred at the juncture between the civilization of settlement and the savagery of wilderness. Turner suggested that the American character was unique and that it came not from European influences but from the presence of a great frontier on our continent, which represented the border between "savagery and civilization." He wrote that the individuals who settled the wilderness embodied the qualities that made America special and superior.[16]

These individuals, called frontiersmen, included both men and women.[17] Adele Lubbock Briscoe Looscan wrote in 1898, "While men are animated by love of adventure, desire for wealth or fame, which convert every obstacle overcome into a glorious triumph, female pioneers are sustained alone by the strength of their devotion to others, and weak hands learn to perform labors, and tender hearts to bear trials, unendurable by the sterner sex, and which in less perilous times would have been impossible, even themselves." As if describing the situation at Camp Verde, Looscan goes on to say, "It requires far less strength of character to face visible danger than to dwell calmly where it is known to be near, but keeps partially veiled."[18]

Verde Valley was an archetype for the manifestation of the frontier. Once through Puerta de Bandera, the environment changed rapidly. Verde Creek flows its entire length in an environment characterized by a plateau with highly localized arroyos and shallow limestone and clay soils that support oak and ash juniper (cedar) woodlands. Early explorers gave the name Valle de Verde, Spanish for "green valley," to this watershed and the name Rio Verde to the modern-day Verde Creek.[19] At the crossing of Rio Verde, the Spanish named a nearby hill Monte del Mesa. Perhaps the Spanish may have known the waypoint at the crossing as El Campo Verde.

1

Prehistoric Verde Valley

Texas prehistory reaches back at least twelve thousand years, as suggested by a large quantity of archaeological evidence. There are more than fifty thousand prehistoric archaeological sites identified across the state of Texas.[20] Within the Verde Creek area, prehistoric artifacts and features are innumerable. Although previous investigations of the prehistoric archaeology of the Verde Valley were cursory, the broader span of ethnohistorical research[21] has provided a valuable source of general information regarding aboriginal settlement patterns in the Verde Valley area.[22]

The record of human occupation of the Verde Valley dates back to the Paleo-Indian people of the Clovis culture some twelve thousand years ago. Clovis points were discovered along the Guadalupe River within twenty miles of the Verde Valley. The distinctive Clovis fluted point is widespread and was used for hunting the Columbian mammoth.[23]

Lithic (rock) resources in the Verde Valley are generally limited to the uplands and hillsides. Edwards chert[24] occurs in the Verde Valley area most frequently at elevations between 1,850 and 2,000 feet. Middens (so-called Indian mounds) are numerous throughout the Verde Creek drainage basin, usually on the second terrace above stream channels. Untold numbers of artifacts (perhaps thousands) have been unofficially collected by landowners and "pot diggers" ever since the Spanish intrusion into this area in the early eighteenth century.

In the summers of 1971 and 1972, the Texas Archeological Society (TAS) conducted field schools in the Turtle Creek Watershed within

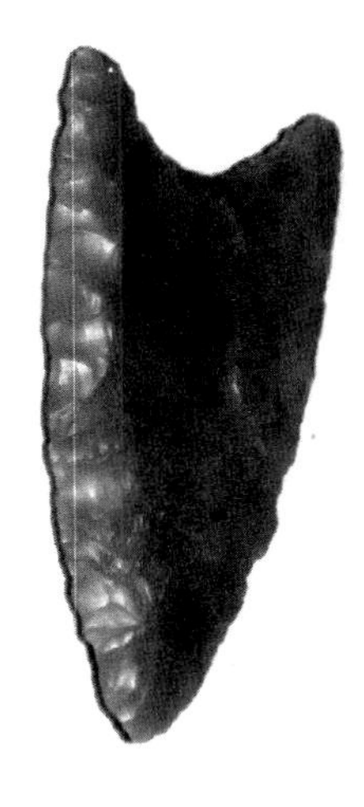

Clovis point. *Photo by author, artifact courtesy of Carol J. Meyer.*

five miles of the Verde Valley.[25] During the two-season survey, 165 prehistoric sites were located and recorded. Archaic occupation sites represent 80 percent of the recorded sites. Archaic and Late Prehistoric components were evident at 12 sites, and uncontaminated Late Prehistoric components were present at the sites. Based on this data, the occupation of the Turtle Creek Watershed is considered Archaic.[26] The Turtle Creek Watershed is assumed to be characteristic of the archaeological condition of the Verde Creek Watershed.

Archaeologists have defined four broad periods of prehistoric human occupation in this region: Paleo-Indian, Archaic, Late Prehistoric and Historic.[27] This chronology is a broadly generalized one drawn largely from *Stone Artifacts of Texas Indians* by Ellen Sue Turner, Thomas R. Hester and Richard L. McReynolds[28] and can be briefly summarized as follows:

Paleo-Indian (11,500–8,000 years ago)
Early Archaic (8,000–4,500 years ago)
Middle Archaic (4,500–3,000 years ago)
Late Archaic and Transitional Archaic (3,000–1,300 years ago)
Late Prehistoric (1,300–300 years ago)

PALEO-INDIAN PEOPLE

Among the first people in the Verde Valley were Paleo-Indians. Texas archaeologists use the term "Paleo-Indian" to refer to the earliest human occupation of the state twelve thousand years BP (before present). A flint projectile point found along Verde Creek might be older than a priceless relic from the First Dynasty in Egypt (five thousand years BP). Knapped (flaked) points and tools are abundant in the Verde Valley. Occupation and kill sites, with associated human artifacts and Pleistocene[29] fauna, have been identified along the Balcones Escarpment. While Paleo-Indian sites with clear evidence of Pleistocene faunal (wildlife) associations are few, the projectile points that distinguish the early part of this period are widespread; these include Clovis, Folsom and Plainview points. Other diagnostic point types are Golondrina, Scottsbluff, Angostura and some highly localized styles still under analysis (see *Stone Artifacts of Texas Indians* for further illustrations and discussions of all these types).[30]

Archaic People

The term "Archaic" is used to denote a long time span of hunting and gathering cultural patterns that began around 8,000 years BP and continued until 1,300 years BP. The Early Archaic (8,000–4,500 years BP) is typified by specific diagnostic dart point types (Bell, Gower, Early Corner-Notched and tool forms, Guadalupe and Clear Fork implements). It is suggested that population densities were low and groups were organized into small, highly mobile bands. Interestingly, many of the key sites of this era are clustered along the edge of the Balcones Escarpment.[31]

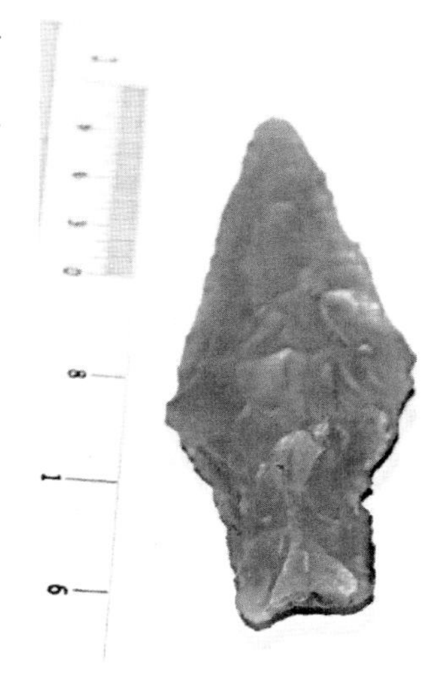

Gower point. *Photo by author.*

The Archaic Period is significant for changes in the style of projectile points and tools, the distribution of site types and the introduction of grinding implements and ground stone ornaments. Projectile points are commonly called arrowheads but are actually dart points used with the atlatl. The primary weapon during the Archaic Period was the spear thrower, or atlatl, as the bow and arrow had not yet been introduced.[32] By far, the largest number of Kerr County archaeological sites reported is categorized as Archaic.[33]

The Gatlin site in Kerrville is located immediately south of the Spur 98 crossing of the Guadalupe River, ten miles from the Verde Valley (30°3.894′N, 99°10.942′W). This significant archaeological site represents one of the largest excavated samples of Early Archaic deposits in the central Texas archaeological region. Located essentially at the gates of the Saddlewood Estates, this site was inhabited as early as seven thousand years ago.[34]

MIDDLE ARCHAIC PEOPLE

The Middle Archaic (4,500–3,000 years BP) was a period of population growth, with the native peoples developing specialized adaptations to the hunting and gathering of abundant regional food resources, especially acorns and white-tailed deer. The Pedernales dart point type is a diagnostic of the period, as are large accumulations of fire-cracked rock known as burned rock middens. Today, in Kerr County, these accumulations of burned rocks are commonly known as Indian mounds; there are as many as ten thousand in Kerr County alone.

Pedernales point. *Photo by author.*

Most of the so-called arrowheads found in this area are really atlatl dart points. This dart is usually six to seven feet in length. This ancient spear thrower used leverage to achieve greater velocity in dart throwing. The atlatl used the same principle as do today's molded plastic shafts for throwing tennis balls for dogs. It consisted of a shaft with a cup or a spur at the end that supported and propelled the butt of the dart. The atlatl was held in one hand, gripped near the end farthest from the cup. The dart was thrown by the action of the upper arm and wrist, using the atlatl as a low-mass, fast-moving extension of the throwing arm. Modern enthusiasts describe the projectile as "an arrow on steroids" capable of traveling eighty to ninety miles per hour.[35]

LATE PREHISTORIC PEOPLE

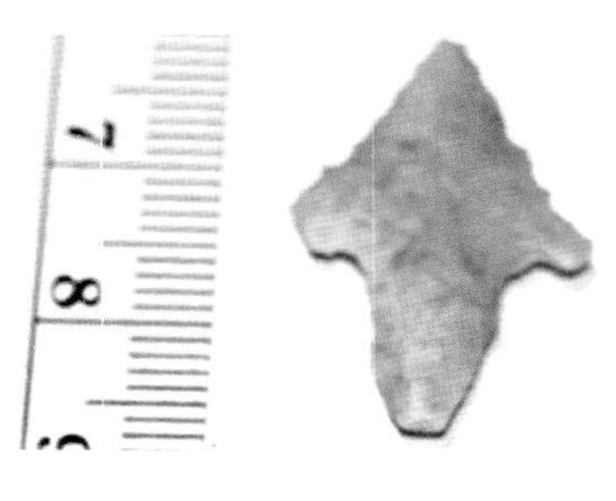

Perdiz point. *Photo by author.*

The Late Prehistoric Period (1,300–300 years BP) was a time of practical adaptation imposed by environmental determinism due to climate change. The most significant change was the introduction of the bow and arrow (about AD 750) and its widespread popularity. The small arrow-

Indians digging irrigating ditches. *Image from* On a Mexican Mustang, Through Texas, from the Gulf to the Rio Grande, *by Alex E. Sweet and J. Armoy Knox, 1883.*

sized projectile point types of this period include Scallorn, Granbury, Perdiz and Cliffton.[36]

The Late Prehistoric Period lasted until the coming of the Spanish.[37] At the end of the Late Prehistoric Period, the aboriginal peoples of the South Texas Plains had lost almost all ethnic identity and were, effectively, culturally extinct. These natives were captured or lured into the Spanish communities that formed around the missions.[38]

Collectively, all these groups have come to be known as Coahuiltecans (kwa-weel-tekens), but they spoke diverse dialects and languages, some of which were distantly related to one another at best. Some of the major languages were Comecrudo, Cotoname, Aranama, Solano, Sanan and Coahuilteco. The term "Coahuiltecan," in its proper sense, is a geographic catchall that could be defined as "the native peoples of south Texas and northeastern Mexico." They may well have been direct linear descendants of the Paleo-Indian peoples who came to the region more than twelve thousand years earlier and whose descendants stayed on.[39]

2

First Contact

The date of the first contact of the Spanish with native peoples in the Verde Valley is unknown but was probably by the late sixteenth century. During the Historic Period (the time of written records, beginning roughly in the mid-1500s in the region), hundreds of groups of native peoples were moving around the area that is now Texas and northern Mexico. Michael Collins has estimated the number of named Indian groups to be close to six hundred, as recorded in documents from early Euro-American settlement of Texas.[40]

Camp Verde seems to have been a significant place of convergence for historic Indians as they traveled the ancient paths (later known as the Apache Trail, the Comanche Trail and the San Saba Trail) to the trade rendezvous held at Ojo de Agua de Guadalupe, the headwaters of the Guadalupe River in western Kerr County (30°3.221′N, 99°32.035′W).

This annual event in central Texas appears to have been the historic Indian equivalent of the modern Texas State Fair. This Hill Country rendezvous acted as a conduit for Spanish horses flowing east and French weaponry, textiles and nonessentials moving west. "Eyewitness accounts of a fair held in the late 1600s noted the exchange of numerous items, including horses, red ochre, deer skins, Osage orange, salt, and European commodities." Apparently, the Hasinais from east Texas imported horses, slaves and mules from the Bidais, a Caddoan community that resided on the lower Trinity River.[41]

Stone arrow points were replaced by metal by the late 1600s. The French and Spanish provided scrap metal as well as trade points. Indians

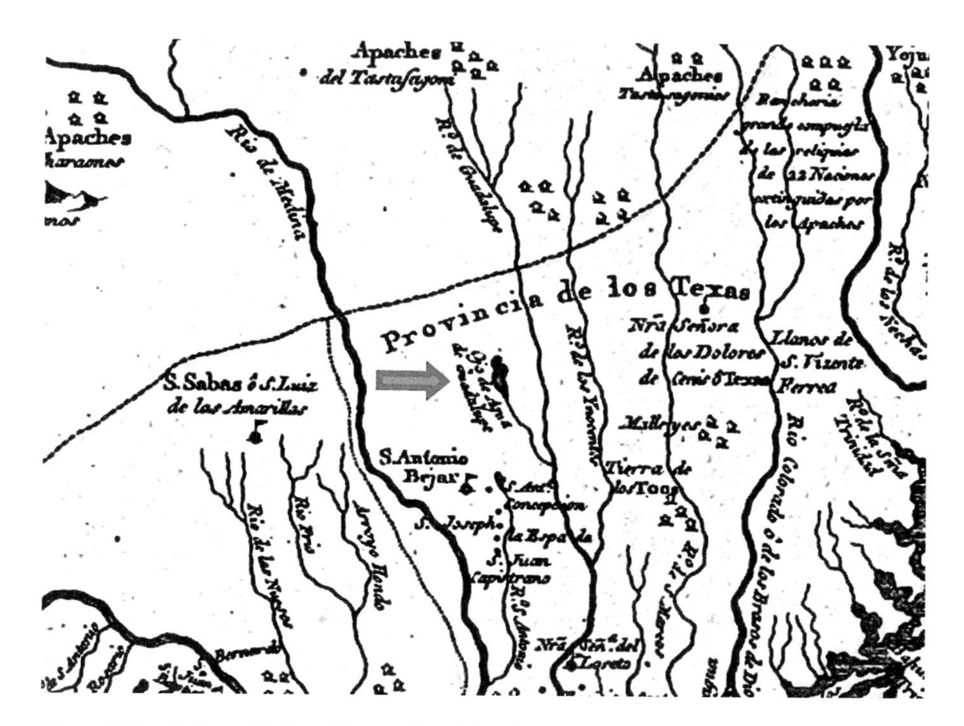

Map of Ojo de Agua de Guadalupe. *Adapted from* Nuevo Mapa Geografico de la America Septentrional, by *José Antonio de Alzate y Ramírez, 1768.*

manufactured weapons and tools from barrel hoops, utensils and wagon parts. They chiseled a point out of a strip of barrel band and then sharpened and refined the arrowhead with a file. Raiders brought home hoops and horses.[42]

According to a French trader from that era, the Hasinais (Caddos) traded guns to the Bidais, who in turn supplied the Apaches. Using these firearms, the Apaches raided Spanish concerns for horses and mules. The Hasinais forged an alliance with the Lipans in 1782. To commemorate this event, the Apaches traded one thousand horses to the Tonkawas, Hasinais and Bidais for 270 firearms.[43]

Aboriginal people of the Verde Valley must have had contact with the Spanish by the time of the establishment of San Antonio. Informal and unofficial scouting may have taken Spanish explorers into the Verde Creek area in search of silver and other sources of wealth. There is a Spanish date of 1577 found carved in a probable mine prospect in Bandera County.[44] With the founding of the Mission San Antonio de

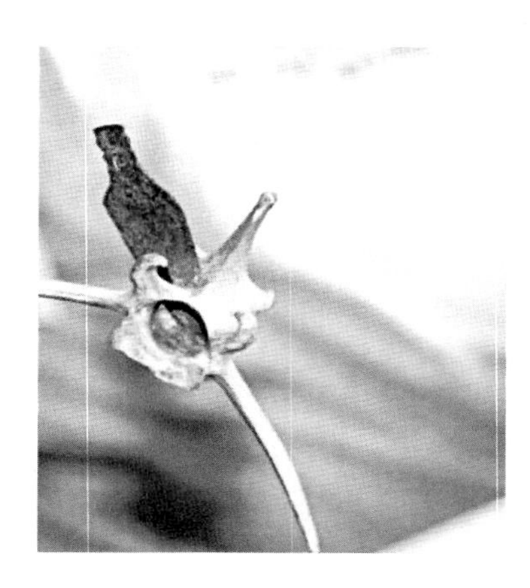

Metal arrow in deer bone. *Photo by author, artifact courtesy of Roy Yeberra.*

Valero (29°25.523′N, 98°29.161′W) in 1718, many of the aboriginal groups living in the San Antonio area were relocated from their traditional environs and concentrated into the San Antonio missions. Many of these aboriginals, clearly displaced from their traditional homelands and decimated by Spanish-introduced diseases, had already lost their pre-contact cultural systems. Artifacts associated with the Historic Contact Period include metal knives, metal arrow points, glass beads, glass, copper kettle fragments and gun parts.[45]

COAHUILTECANS

Noted archaeologist Tom Hester comments that Indians in this part of Texas are often incorrectly referred to as "Coahuiltecans." He goes on to say, "There never was a Coahuiltecan culture." There were some Coahuilteco speakers, but by the time the Spanish arrived in Texas, most of the local peoples had been pushed out by non-Coahuilteco speakers fleeing Spanish diseases in northeastern Mexico.[46]

In the San Antonio region, the Franciscans mainly encountered bands of hunter-gatherers the Spanish called Coahuiltecos, or Coahuiltecans. A large number of the so-called Coahuiltecans gathered in Spanish missions for protection from the Apaches. By 1800, most of the remaining Coahuiltecans had merged with other tribes or intermarried with the Hispanic population.[47]

These so-called Coahuiltecans had only a few tools and weapons. These aboriginals lived in small huts made of bent saplings covered with reed mats or hides. Curved sticks served as all-purpose tools. Gourds rather than ceramic pots provided storage for mesquite or sotol flour and water. Large net bags made of plant fibers held most of the things that were transported from place to place. The bow and arrow was their primary weapon.[48]

Jumanos

Jumano is the name given to three distinct groups who ranged over northern Mexico, New Mexico and Texas. During the Spanish years, the Jumanos were effective in organizing trade fairs between the Spanish and other tribes. The Jumanos sometimes acted as scouts for the Spanish. During the last decades of the seventeenth century, Spaniards from Coahuila encountered mounted Jumanos at locations including the Guadalupe River. By 1700, the Jumanos had lost all their territory and trade routes. Their culture eventually died out, with the survivors drifting to join other tribes, including the Apaches. Some scholars believe that a small group of Jumanos became the foundation of the Kiowas in Texas.[49]

Payayas

The Payayas (Paia, Paialla, Payai, Payagua, Payata, Piyai and other variants) were a Coahuiltecan-speaking group first reported about 1690. They lived and hunted in the Verde Valley area. This tribe originally ranged across an area that extended from San Antonio southwestward to the Frio River and beyond. However, it is with the San Antonio area that the Payayas were most consistently associated. A local stream was referred to as El Arroyo de los Payayas, and a pass through the hills northwest of Boerne was known as Puerta de los Payayas (also known as Spanish Pass).[50] Yanaguana, the Payaya name for the San Antonio River, has been preserved and is perpetuated by the Yanaguana Society of San Antonio. The Payayas joined missions in both Coahuila and Texas. The Payaya Indians were one of the groups for whom the San Antonio de Valero Mission was established in the area of present-day San Antonio in 1718, and they are mentioned in records of this mission as late as 1776. Some Payayas were also at nearby Nuestra Señora de la Purísima Concepción de Acuña Mission.[51]

Tonkawas

The Tonkawas arrived in central Texas around 1680 from a homeland in Oklahoma. "Tonkawa Indians" was actually the name given to several

Tonkawa Indians. *By Lino Sanchez y Tapia, 1828.*

independent groups that banded together in the Kerr County region of central Texas in the early 1700s.[52] The Tonkawas are most closely linked to the Verde Valley.[53] They were nomadic buffalo hunters. Over time, they became traditional enemies of the Apaches. They resisted Spanish colonization and played a leading role in the destruction of the Santa Cruz de San Sabá Mission near present-day Menard.[54]

The Tonkawas were formidable warriors who possessed a reputation for cannibalism. Most anthropologists feel that the concept of the Tonkawas as cannibals came from their ritual eating of flesh from the bodies of their slain enemies.[55] Literature, such as that written by Andree J. Sjoberg ("The Culture of the Tonkawa, A Texas Indian Tribe," *Texas Journal of Science*, 1953) and Robert Hasskarl ("The Culture and History of the Tonkawa Indians," *Plains Anthropologist*, November 1962), contains some useful information on Tonkawa ethnology. These ethnologies provide a picture of a tribe that occupied the transitional zone between Plains Indian culture and the desert culture of south Texas.[56]

3
Spanish Texas

The Verde Valley was situated in Spanish Texas for 131 years. Given that the Spanish named landmarks in the immediate vicinity, more than likely this was an important waypoint on the Spanish Trail west and may have been named El Campo Verde. Old maps show one nearby hill that was named Monte del Mesa—today's Cedar Ridge (29°53.195′N, 99°7.184′W).[57]

Spanish Texas was one of the interior provinces of New Spain from 1690 until 1821. Although Spain claimed ownership of the territory, the Spanish did not attempt to colonize the area until after discovering evidence of LaSalle's failed French colony of Fort Saint Louis[58] in 1689.

The Encomienda

Some ethnohistorians denigrate the Spanish colonial motivation. Newcomb writing about the historic setting of the Lipan Mission of San Lorenzo de la Santa Cruz at the headwaters of the Nueces River is one such example. He writes, "This was a bloody, ruthless conquest; if the native peoples could not be enslaved, they were exterminated."[59] The basis of this enslavement policy was the Spanish colonial encomienda. In this policy, the crown granted a person a certain number of slaves for whom they were to take responsibility. The Spaniards were to "protect the natives from warring tribes, and to instruct them in the Spanish language and in the Catholic faith; in return they could extract tribute from the natives in the form of labor, gold or other products."[60]

The process of the encomienda, called "reduction" of the natives, often involved brutal practices. One history of the era notes, "When these holy men failed to persuade the Indians to adopt their religious views, they put them in a persuasive instrument called 'a virgin.'" Essentially a medieval torture instrument, this instrument was an iron container, body shaped, that closely fitted the Indian's body like an Egyptian mummy. It could be screwed together tighter and tighter, compressing the entire body. "That was how the Indians were reduced. Eight out of every ten of those treated to the virgin were converted." The other two died.[61]

Missions and Presidios

Over the years, Spain established numerous villages, missions and forts in the province. A small number of Spanish settlers arrived, in addition to missionaries and soldiers. Spain signed agreements with colonizers from the United States.[62] In New Spain, a *mestizo* was a person born in the New World with one Spanish-born and one Indian parent. Many Tejanos were descendants of mestizos. On the frontier, this group rapidly became the largest segment of the population. In the colonial caste system of Spanish America, a *peninsular* was a Spanish-born Spaniard or mainland Spaniard residing in the New World. A *criollo* was a person born in the New World to Spanish-born parents. A criollo, although legally equal to a peninsular, was treated differently with regard to royal appointments to high colonial offices in administration, the military and the church. The stigma of being born in America emerged from the difficulty of distinguishing between pure criollos and mestizos. The highest offices were usually reserved for the Spanish-born peninsulars, and criollos and mestizos shared the other military and civil appointments.[63]

At times, modern Texas was part of four provinces within the vast kingdom of New Spain: the El Paso area was under the jurisdiction of New Mexico; missions founded near the confluence of the Río Conchos and Río Grande (La Junta de los Ríos) were under Nueva Vizcaya; the coastal region from the Nueces River to the Río Grande and thence upstream to Laredo fell under Nuevo Santander after 1749; and Tejas, initially known as the "New Kingdom of the Philippines," was briefly

(1694–1715) under joint jurisdiction with Coahuila. The Verde Valley was situated in the area that formally constituted the Spanish province of Tejas.[64]

Near San Pedro Springs (29°27′N, 98°30′W), Martín de Alarcón founded San Antonio de Valero Mission[65] and San Antonio de Béxar (or Béjar) Presidio in May 1718.[66] The five Béxar missions, together with the presidio and the villa of San Fernando, constituted the most important Spanish concentration in Texas. By the mid-1730s, the total population of the area was some nine hundred, including three hundred Spanish and six hundred Indian converts.[67] Spanish activities during this period may have reached to Leon Springs, La Puerta de Las Casas Viejas (29°39′N, 98°38′W), as well as Helotes, Puerta de Los Elotes (29°35′N, 98°41′W).

A band of Apaches attacked two men at Puerta de Los Elotes in 1723. One was killed, and the other escaped back to the presidio. Upon hearing this report, Captain Nicholas Flores immediately sent out an alfrez (lieutenant) with fifteen men. The soldiers found the body of the Spaniard, "who had been scalped and shot through with many arrows."[68]

The Spanish in Texas had insignificant contact with the Apaches in the decades prior to 1730. After that year, the number of contacts gradually increased. Gerald Betty, in his book on Comanche society, attributes this development to the continuation of the Comanche push southward.[69]

José de Urrutia

Here was the heroic Spanish frontiersman, living and fighting on the brink of civilization in Spanish Texas. He had entered Tejas in 1691, lived among the Indians for seven years, was made captain general of all the nations hostile to the Apaches, conducted several extensive campaigns with these tribes against the Apaches and eventually became captain and commander of the presidio of San Antonio de Béxar. Urrutia crossed the frontier, recorded the existence of Puerta de Bandera and conducted Spanish campaigns against the Apaches on the upper Guadalupe, Llano and San Saba Rivers.

José de Urrutia was born in Guipúzcoa, Spain, about 1678, thus was a peninsular and eligible for the highest offices in New Spain. Urrutia was a member of the first Spanish expedition to explore the San Antonio region. He came with an expedition in 1691 led by Domingo Terán de los Ríos[70] and Fray Damián Massanet,[71] who evidently reached the San Antonio River near where the San Juan Capistrano Mission was later founded. Urrutia was a mere youth at the time. Nearby, the expedition encountered a clan of Payaya Indians living on the riverbank. Massanet named the site San Antonio de Padua to celebrate the memorial day of St. Anthony, June 13.

In 1691, Domingo Terán de los Rios renamed today's Guadalupe River the San Agustin.[72] For a time, maps showed it as the Rio Alarcón. The river was generally called the Nuestra Señora de Guadalupe, as named by Alonso De León in 1689. Many explorers referred to the current Guadalupe as the San Ybón above its confluence with the Comal, and instead the Comal was called the Guadalupe.[73]

At first, the Spanish promoted missions and presidios in eastern Texas and Louisiana to counter the French threat as manifested by LaSalle. Therefore, the early capital of Spanish Texas, and the Kerr County region, was at Los Adaes in what is now western Louisiana.[74] The Tejas Indians in east Texas turned hostile, forcing the garrison into a tortuous withdrawal from Texas. When the Spanish pulled out in 1693, Urrutia was injured and remained among the Indians. He lived with the Kanohatinos, Tohos and Xarames, serving as captain general of all the nations hostile to the Apaches. In this command, José de Urrutia conducted numerous extensive campaigns against the Apaches over seven years.[75]

By July 23, 1733, José de Urrutia was the consummate heroic frontiersman of Spanish Texas. He had forty years' experience with the Indians in Coahuila, Nuevo León and Texas and was probably the most knowledgeable on Indian affairs of all the New World Spaniards. He earned the commission as captain and commander of the Presidio de San Antonio de Béxar.[76]

The Apaches raided San Antonio relentlessly from 1736 to 1739, killing several soldiers and settlers. Captain José de Urrutia of the Presidio de San Antonio de Béxar pressed for a new campaign against the Indians. In the winter of 1739, his force sortied from San Antonio for the San Sabá. Urrutia's men discovered Puerta de Bandera, through which the Apaches made their forays. After crossing Rio Verde, they pressed on directly to the San Sabá River country, where they surprised an Indian camp and seized a large number of captives. Urrutia apparently took the shortest possible route to the place where the town of Menard now stands, near the restored Presidio de San Luis de las Amarillas, and returned the same way.[77] El Campo Verde was a likely overnight stop on this trek.

Captain José de Urrutia's recommendation for a presidio at Rio Verde, presumably to guard the pass, was ignored. The shorter, though perilous, Puerta de Bandera route provided faster communication between Béxar and the mission outpost of San Sabá.

Toribio de Urrutia

Toribio de Urrutia followed his father as captain of the San Antonio de Béxar Presidio, and in 1743, he was justicia mayor of San Antonio. Conditions at San Antonio had become so bad that citizens could neither take the road for Coahuila nor work in their fields except in large parties. Captain Toribio de Urrutia, son of the former captain, desired to undertake another campaign but was strongly opposed by the missionaries, who were now trying to bring peace to the province by founding an Apache mission.[78]

At last, in 1745, after much delay, Toribio de Urrutia secured permission from the authorities and made the expedition. Urrutia, in command of some fifty Spaniards, led a punitive campaign against the Apaches. The expedition may have again probed as far as the San Saba River and probably marched through the Puerta de Bandera used by his father. In a clash with Lipans and other Apaches, Urrutia defeated the Indians and took a number of them captive.

As conquistadors realized that full suits of armor were overkill in the New World, some of them switched to lighter chainmail, which was just as effective. Some even abandoned metal armor entirely, wearing escuapil, a sort of padded leather or cloth armor adapted from the armor worn by Aztec warriors.

On February 2, 1749, Captain Urrutia, with some two hundred men, most of them being Indian allies, again set out toward Apache country. The 1749 expedition marched from San Antonio along the Apache Trail through Puerta de Bandera to the banks of the Upper Guadalupe River, probably to Ojo de Agua de Guadalupe, the headwaters (30°3.221′N, 99°32.035′W). This appears to be the same La Rivera ranchería that was home to Cuero de Coyote in 1740.[79] The Spanish attacked the camp, expecting some four hundred enemies. Since most of the Lipan warriors were out on a buffalo hunt, the Spanish captured only fifty men, ninety women and forty-seven children.[80] Dunn states that the rationale for this attack was the presence of valuable minerals in the San Saba area.[81]

Spanish soldier. *By Ramon de Murilla, 1804.*

These Apaches were captured and carried to San Antonio, where the men were imprisoned and the women and children placed in the safekeeping of the citizens and the missionaries, with orders to treat them with the greatest kindness but not to let them escape.[82]

THE SAN SABA—APACHE TRAIL

The San Saba Trail originated near the Ojo de Agua San Pedro, today's San Pedro Springs[83] in San Antonio (29°26.797′N, 98°30.102′W), and proceeded in a general northwesterly direction along the route of present-day Highway 16 (Bandera Highway). Traversing Puerta de Elotes (29°35.204′N, 98°41.766′W) near Helotes, the route continued through to San Geronimo, Pipe Creek, to today's town of Bandera (29°43.491′N, 99°4.241′W). The trail then turned northward, generally following the present-day Highway 173 through the Puerta de Bandera (29°51.808′N,

99°6.408′W) to the present site of Camp Verde (29°33′N, 98°46′W). West of Camp Verde, the trail passed Monteverde (Mount Verde) and crossed Puerta de Verde (29°55.083′N, 99°6.66′W). At Kerrville, the trail crossed the Guadalupe River just above the confluence with today's Town Creek (30°2.963′N, 99°9.226′W), proceeding in a northwesterly direction along the Guadalupe River to present-day Ingram. The trail then generally followed the route of Highway 27 along today's Johnson Creek to modern Mountain Home. Here, the trail reached the divide, a relatively level area of rolling hills. This area is where IH-10 now extends between Kerrville and Junction, and the San Saba Trail generally followed the path of this present-day highway.

A few miles east of Junction, the trail reached the site of what was to become Segovia (30°25.092′N, 99°40.179′W). Nearby, a state historical marker indicates that this was the military route to Fort Terrett and Fort McKavett. From Segovia, the trail followed today's Ranch Road 2169 and the Johnson Fork of the Llano River past a high bluff known as Cloud Point (30°29.69′N, 99°41.876′W). Then the trail crossed the Llano River north of modern Junction and turned northward in general alignment with U.S. 83 toward the area of the present-day city of Menard, where the Presidio San Luis de las Amarillas was located (30°55.365′N, 99°48.187′W).

Another Spanish trail crossed western Kerr County between the Presidio de San Juan Bautista on the Rio Grande and the Presidio of San Luis de las Amarillas. Blazed by Felipe de Rabago y Teran in 1760, this route went to the headwaters of the Nueces River and then crossed both the south and north forks of the Guadalupe River on its way to the San Saba.[84] This trail is shown on Lafora's 1771 map.[85]

Historically, another old trail—Camino Pinta—ran through the natural pass (La Puerta de Las Casas Viejas) formed by the Leon Creek Valley. Pinta was the name of a Lipan Apache chief of that area.[86] In the early history of the Béxar settlement, the historical trail also may have been called the Camino de Tehuacanas (an apparent reference to the Tawakonis, a Wichita group commonly associated with north central Texas throughout the eighteenth century).[87]

APACHE RELATIONS

At the beginning of August 1749, it was reported that there were encamped on the Guadalupe four Apache chiefs with one hundred followers of each headman. These chiefs came with the intention of obtaining peace and their captive relatives. They said they would wait on the Guadalupe until the Spaniards should appoint a day for them to enter the settlement. Captain Urrutia received them with all consideration and supplied them with presents. The Spanish told them to return to the Guadalupe and tell their chiefs to come whenever they pleased but to use smoke as a signal before starting so that they could be properly received. On August 19, 1749, the four Apache chiefs, with numerous followers, buried a hatchet, along with other instruments of war, in a remarkable peace ceremony at San Antonio.[88]

The Spanish missionaries, guard troops and settlers assembled on the plaza in San Antonio. In addition, there were Indian chiefs, their people and prisoners. The Apaches dug a large pit in the middle of the plaza in which they placed a living horse, a hatchet (war club), a lance and six arrows. The chiefs held hands with Toribio de Urrutia at the edge of the pit, dancing three times around it. The same dance was done with the missionaries and settlers. When all was buried, the Apaches believed they had buried war (buried the hatchet).[89]

The missionaries proposed that an Apache mission be located on the Guadalupe River, about forty-five miles northeast of the Béxar Presidio (approximate distance to Verde Creek via Puerta de Bandera), "where the Lipan rancherias were already located." The president of the Texas missions, Father Santa Ana, recommended a site, in 1750, on the Pedernales River (Guadalupe?),[90] some sixty miles northwest of the Béxar Presidio. This is the approximate distance to today's Kerrville. Father Santa Ana's proposal that Puerta de Bandera could control the movement of the Apaches bespoke the significance of the Verde Valley frontier.[91]

SANTA CRUZ DE SAN SABÁ MISSION

The Franciscan missionaries at San Antonio proposed several plans to set up missions for the Apaches. Seeking to place a mission closer to Apache territory and the potential for silver mining in the region of San Sabá, which was located in the heart of Apachería, made a convincing argument for that location at present-day Menard. After visiting Cerro Del Almagre and Los Almagres, Bernardo de Miranda y Flores, in his 1756 report to the Spanish provincial governor, said there was "enough for every person to own a silver mine."[92]

Miranda was convinced that silver-bearing ore could be extracted in large quantities because of the extent of iron oxide rock he observed. The prospect of silver mines became the basis for the establishment of the mission and presidio at today's Menard. Historians note that Jim Bowie found a "lost silver mine" at Los Almagres. The lure of these silver prospects has continued to draw adventurers to the area, even today.[93]

Intent on establishing the mission, Fray Alonso Giraldo Terreros, Captain Don Diego Ortiz Parrilla and their entourage followed the old trail through Puerta de Bandera and along the Guadalupe River to reach the Rio San Saba.[94] When this expedition arrived in April 1757, they found no Indians to greet them. Still, despite Parrilla's objections, the missionaries demanded that construction begin, and Parrilla yielded to their pressure. The mission and presidio (fortification) were built several miles apart.[95]

In June 1757, the first Indians began to arrive at the site, and within days, three thousand Apaches were encamped around the mission. The missionaries were overjoyed until they learned that the Indians were not willing to enter the mission. The Apaches had gathered here for their annual buffalo hunt and for a campaign against their enemies, the northern tribes. The Indians soon departed, promising to return to settle at the mission upon completion of their hunt.

Armageddon arrived on March 16, 1758. A party of two thousand Comanche, Tejas, Bidai, Tonkawa and other Indians swooped down on the Santa Cruz de San Sabá Mission, massacred the inhabitants, pillaged the supplies and burned the buildings. When the Indians attacked the mission, the presidio, with its soldiers dispersed on various assignments, was powerless to intervene.[96]

Consequently, Parrilla was assigned elsewhere. Felipe de Rábago y Terán took command of the presidio of San Saba. When Terán departed Coahuila to take up his new post, he blazed a new trail directly from San Juan Bautista on the Rio Grande to the San Saba Presidio, completely bypassing San Antonio. The new trail from San Juan Bautista to Presidio San Saba crossed the headwaters of the Nueces, Frio and Guadalupe Rivers, as shown on Lafora's map of 1771.[97]

This fresh trail presented geographical opportunities to locate new missions on the upper Nueces River. This resulted in the development of

Santa Cruz de San Saba Presidio. *Photo by author.*

two new missions, San Lorenzo de la Santa Cruz (present-day Camp Wood, 29°40.114'N, 100°061'W) and Nuestra Senora de la Candelaria (near present-day Montell, 29°32.301'N, 100°0466'W). The Lipan chief Cavezon, with a band of three hundred people, settled at the Santa Cruz site.[98]

After March 1761, the Presidio de San Luis de las Amarillas, at today's Menard, was rebuilt as a very strong stone fortification and was renamed Real Presidio de San Saba. It was completed in 1761 and stands today as a remarkable and rare example of European stone fortification, complete with turrets, arched gates and crenellated battlements along the tops of the walls.[99] Today, the presidio is in the process of restoration.[100]

NICOLÁS DE LAFORA

Nicolás de Lafora, soldier and explorer, was selected in 1766 by the Marqués de Cruillas, the viceroy of New Spain, to accompany the Marqués de Rubí's massive inspection of the northern frontier of New Spain. By Lafora's own estimate, he traveled 2,936 leagues (approximately 7,600 miles) over a span of twenty-three months. His specific responsibilities included recording day-by-day information on physical features, geographical coordinates and ethnographic information. Aside from these obligations, he was to assist in compiling maps. On his own initiative, he wrote a descriptive account of the provinces of Nueva Vizcaya, New Mexico, Sonora, Nuevo León, Coahuila, Texas, New Galicia and Nayarit. That narrative, in the words of Lawrence Kinnaird, "is the best single source of information upon the frontiers of New Spain yet found."[101]

Maps of this era are confusing, as the geographic names of many places and geographic features have changed over times, and in some cases cartographic mistakes have been made. This is particularly true for the area of the Upper Guadalupe River. Verde Creek was known to the Spanish as Rio Verde. In Nicholas Lafora's 1771 map of Texas, the Upper Guadalupe River was named Rio de Alarcón, including the north and south forks. Johnson Creek was mistakenly named Rio de Pedernales.[102]

Nicholas de Lafora's map of 1771. *Adapted from Nicolas de Lafora's map of 1771,* Mapa de toda la frontera de los dominios del rey en la America Septentrional. *Original map in the Ministerio del Ejerite Servicio Geografico, Session Topografia, Madrid.*

Spanish Heritage

The Spanish had extensive involvement in the Hill Country. Due to the portal at Puerta de Bandera, many expeditions seem to have passed through the Verde Valley. The Guadalupe River, approached from both Puerta de Bandera and Puerta de los Payayas (Spanish Pass), was a major route to the north and west. Although no Spanish land grants appear in Kerr County, there are likely many artifacts and features to be found. Archaeologists and historians would do well to investigate with metal detectors.

4

The Lipan Apaches

Náizhan

The Apache did not arrive in the Verde Valley area until after the Spanish were in San Antonio. An Apache tribe, designating themselves Náizhan ("ours" or "our kind"), ranged through Texas, raiding and looting other tribes, as well as the Spanish and Euro-American settlements of Texas and Mexico. These "Eastern Apaches" were called the Lipan Apache.[103] Lipan (adapted from Ipa-nde) is apparently a personal name (nde=people).[104]

As soon as the Apaches learned of the establishment of Béxar, they began to badger it. By 1720, the Spanish government maintained more soldiers in Béxar than had been employed throughout the conquest and subjugation of the Aztec and Inca empires.[105] The Spanish named the Hill Country around Camp Verde as "Lomeria Grande." The Spanish described the region as "a very broken country." All the country west of the Balcones Escarpment was regarded as Apachería and hostile. The words "Lomeria" and "Apachería" became synonymous.[106]

The Lipan Apache occupied present-day Kerr County for nearly two hundred years. Once the Lipans moved into this area in the 1720s, they established a territorial claim over these lands. "The Apache concept of dominion meant that all resources within their domain became objects to be 'harvested' when needed—including buffalo, deer and even cactus pads or 'tunas.' When the Spanish arrived in the San Antonio region, all horses, cattle, food, material items or Spanish women or children were, by their very presence, resources available for Lipan 'harvest' during a raid."[107]

OJO DE AGUA DE GUADALUPE

In what is now Kerr County were located a number of Apache rancherias (the Spanish term for small Indian settlements) from which these warriors would raid the settlements in and around San Antonio. By 1728, the Lipans were occupying the area immediately north of San Antonio.[108] A large Apache camp was located at Ojo de Agua de Guadalupe, the headwaters of the Guadalupe River (30°3.2′N, 99°32′W).[109] This headwaters camp dates back to prehistory and was the site of many encampments, intertribal trade rendezvous and battles with other tribes, the Spanish, the Texans and the army. Another encampment is shown on a map of Spanish Texas as being located between Puerta de Bandera and Verde Creek to the north, a distance of less than three miles. Most likely, the camp was located on the second terrace on the south bank of Verde Creek, across from today's Camp Verde Store (29°54′N, 99°06′W). The Apache Trail used Puerta de Bandera to raid into San Antonio and the coastal plain of Texas.

THE LIPAN APACHE WARRIOR

Several eyewitness accounts of the Lipan Apaches are available. Of locality relevance is Frank M. Buckelew's tale of capture in 1866 and subsequent life among the Lipans.[110] Another is Herman Lehmann's *Nine Years among the Indians, 1870–1879*.[111] Clinton L. Smith and Jeff D. Smith wrote an account of their life as captives of the Comanches and Apaches.[112] Also of note is Berlandier's *The Indians of Texas in 1830*, which contains his detailed notes of travels through the Kerr County area and the character of the Lipan Apaches.[113] This report is augmented by his traveling companion, José Francisco Ruiz, who wrote a report on the Indian tribes of Texas in 1828.[114]

In September 1731, the Lipan Apaches declared war on the Spaniards at Béxar and revealed the difference between Lipan raiding and Lipan warfare. More than five hundred warriors, each well armed with bows, arrows and metal-tipped lances, stole some fifty horses and then ambushed the pursuing Spanish soldiers. A hard-fought battle between the soldiers and the Indians took place just outside San Antonio. The Apache battle

Apache warrior. *Watercolor by Frederich Richard Petri, circa 1850s.*

tactic was to draw out the Spanish by stealing horses, leading the troops on a chase into an ambush. Once caught in the ambush, the Spanish soldiers faced a much larger force of Apaches, all on horseback and well armed. The Apache warriors would dismount, forming a battle line in the shape of a crescent, eventually enclosing the soldiers. Although excellent horsemen, the Lipan Apaches fought on foot. Warriors would ride to the site of the battle and then dismount to engage their enemy.[115]

The Lipan Apache warrior averaged between five-foot-eight and five-foot-ten in height. He usually wore a buckskin shirt, leggings and knee-high moccasins. In cool weather, he wore a buckskin jacket or buffalo skin. His shirt was beaded and decorated with fringe. Typically, the Lipan warrior was mounted on horseback, using a wooden Spanish-style saddle with iron stirrups. The Lipan warhorses wore armor—a buffalo hide wrapped around the horses' chests to protect the animals from arrows. The main weapon of choice of the Lipan was the bow and arrow. Bows were made of "cedar wood or winter savory sticks." Later, the Lipans used mulberry wood for their bows. Arrows were generally constructed of any "hard, firm wood, which was well-seasoned and always kept in a dry place."[116] Buckelew reported that the Lipans "sometimes poisoned the arrows they used in battle, which if they did not kill a person instantly, the poison would kill the victim in a few days."[117]

The Lipan warriors were renowned for their lances. Buckelew provides a description: "The lance was a long dangerous looking weapon, made of fine steel, and the blade being fastened to a wooden handle with a nice brass ferrule."[118] Berlandier stated that the lance was "usually tipped with the straight blade of a Spanish saber, 2½ feet or so in length, with a shaft 8 or 9 feet long."[119]

The Lipan warrior effectively used a shield in battle. The only description of a Lipan shield comes from Buckelew.[120] Lipan shields were made from thick, untanned bull hide, which was cut in an oval, soaked in water and shaped by placing it in a shallow hole to dry. When the hide had dried, it was ready to be made into a shield. Two slits were cut in each side. A loop of buckskin was placed in the slits and drawn together. Small holes were punched in the edge, and a drawstring was run through these. It was drawn up and evenly tied.[121]

Berlandier acknowledged that the Lipans were "skilled at warfare" but also noted, "Their cruelty is so hideous as would never be accepted as historic fact. They kill their prisoners with the most frightful tortures."[122] Only one reference records the ritual cannibalism practiced by the Lipan

Apache medicine men. *By Koba, 1875. Image courtesy of the Smithsonian National Anthropological Archives.*

Apache. Father Juan Agustin de Morfi, a Spanish historian in Texas in 1778–79, provides a gruesome description of the practice, in which prisoners are slowly tortured and then eaten.[123]

Cabellos Colorados

Cabellos Colorados (Red Hair), a Lipan Apache chief, figured prominently in a raid on San Antonio just after the establishment of the villa by the Canary Islanders in 1731. His band seized citizens in raids. He stole horses from the San Francisco de la Espada Mission and killed Indians from the missions of San Juan Capistrano and Nuestra Señora de la Purísima Concepción de Acuña. After numerous raids in 1736 and 1737, the Spanish captured this Lipan chief on December 11, 1737, and imprisoned him at Béxar until October 1738, when Apache depredations were renewed. He was subsequently sent as a prisoner to Mexico City, where he died.[124]

Camp of the Lipans. *By Theodore Gentilz, 1840s.*

CUERO DE COYOTE

A Lipan Apache chief named Cuero de Coyote visited Toribio de Urrutia in 1731 expressing a desire to settle at the headwaters of the Upper Guadalupe River, about twenty-five leagues (sixty-five miles) above San Antonio.[125] By 1738, Cuero de Coyote was living in a large Apache camp at the site, now known as the "Boneyard" (30°03′N, 99°32′W), adjacent to Ojo de Agua de Guadalupe, the headwaters of the Guadalupe River.

LA RIVERA

A meeting between the Apaches and the Tonkawas was held at a Lipan Apache encampment named La Rivera at Ojo de Agua de Guadalupe during the months of November and December 1782. It was a trade rendezvous. More than two thousand Apaches arrived with three thousand horses. They were met by six hundred Tonkawas and about three hundred Tejas, Bidais, Cocos and Mayeyes. The Tejas and the Bidais brought some two hundred guns to trade. During the two-month trade fair, more than four thousand head of beef cattle were consumed, their bones lying about in great piles.[126] This site on the headwaters of the Guadalupe is located at the Boneyard Crossing near the entrance to the Kerr Wildlife Management Area.[127] The name "Boneyard" derives from the skeletal remains of the four thousand cattle butchered at this site. Writing in the September 15, 1991 issue of the *Kerrville Daily Times*, Mike Bowlin reported that this site was the "last permanent Indian campground in Kerr County." Bowlin went on to note that Indian artifacts dating back ten thousand years were found at or near this site.[128]

Cuelgas de Castro

Cuelgas de Castro was an early to mid-nineteenth-century Lipan chief who inhabited the San Antonio and south Texas region. In 1838, he signed a treaty of friendship and mutual aid between his people and the Republic of Texas. Castro fought with the ranger companies commanded by John Coffee Hays. Castro died in 1842, and his son Juan became chief. Juan Castro served as a leading representative for the Indians on the Brazos Indian Reservation in the 1850s. Rather than accept removal to Indian Territory in 1859, the Lipans fled to Mexico and joined the Kickapoos.[129]

Flacco

Chief Flacco led a Lower Lipan band that ranged from east of San Antonio to areas southwest of San Antonio (particularly Medina and Uvalde Counties). Chief Flacco and his warriors played a vital role in the defense of the new Republic. From 1838 to 1840, they joined Texas militia units led by Stephen Moore in campaigns against the Comanches.[130] Chief Flacco's closest association with the Texans was his relationship with John "Jack" Coffee Hays. Hays described the chief as "tall and erect, with well-shaped limbs. He gave an impression of bounding elasticity. His circlet of eagle feathers was set back on his forehead so that it revealed his black eyes and gave to his bearing a fierce alertness coupled with strength and agility. Flacco's general appearance was suggestive of the hawk and the panther." The Texas Ranger also credited Flacco with saving his life on several occasions in battles against the Comanches.[131]

THE LAST RAID

The last Lipan Apache raid in Kerr County occurred near Center Point in 1876. For the Apaches, this was just another skirmish in a conflict lasting more than 150 years, ever since the Apache had come to the Hill Country early in the eighteenth century.[132]

After 1881, there were no serious attempts on the part of the Lipan Apaches to remain in Texas. Their identity as a distinct people began to fade.[133] Virtually exterminated by smallpox, starvation and relentless warfare, the Lipans had dwindled to a small number by 1900.

Lipan Apache descendants presently live among the Mescalero Apache in New Mexico and the Tonkawa and Plains Apache in Oklahoma. The Lipans are not a federally recognized tribe, and little of their culture remains.[134]

Today, the Lipan Apache Band of Texas membership consists of 745 members and is composed of the Cúelcahén Ndé (People of the Tall Grass), Tú é diné Ndé (Tough People of the Desert), Tú sìs Ndé (Big Water People), Tas steé be glui Ndé (Rock Tied to Head People), Buií gl un Ndé (Many Necklaces People) and Zuá Zuá Ndé (People of the Lava Beds), who have continuously lived in Texas prior to first contact with the Spanish.[135]

5

The Penateka Comanches

The ancestors of the Texas Comanches were the historic Shoshone of California, Idaho, Nevada, Utah and Wyoming. They were of the Uto-Aztecan linguistic stock, a Native American language family consisting of over thirty languages. The Comanche language and the Shoshoni language are quite similar. The Comanches became apparent as a definite group shortly before 1700, when they broke off from the Shoshone people living along the upper Platte River in Wyoming. This divergence coincided with their possession of the horse.[136]

The horse was a fundamental ingredient in the manifestation of a distinctive Comanche culture. Some scholars have suggested the Comanches broke away from the Shoshone and moved southward to search for additional sources of horses among the settlers of New Spain in New Mexico. The Comanche may have been the first group of Plains natives to fully incorporate the horse into their culture and to introduce the animal to the other Plains peoples.[137]

The horse also appears to be the basis of competition for resources carried out by the Comanches. David G. Burnet wrote in 1824, "As the Comanchees [*sic*] do not cultivate the ground, but derive their subsistence from the spontaneous productions of nature, and chiefly from the animal kingdom, they are necessarily migratory, and obliged to change their encampment every ten or fifteen days."[138] The Comanches fought the Apaches for horses and for water and pasture to sustain their horses. The Comanches were the only tribe to engage in combat from horseback; all other Plains Indians dismounted before fighting.

The Comanches ranged throughout Comancheria in search of horses and sufficient grass and water to care for them. A particular locale could be quickly "grazed off" and rendered inadequate for pasturage. This circumstance was particularly critical due to the large number of horses possessed by the Comanches. Gerald Betty, in his book on Comanche society, states, "The daily maintenance of their animals probably encouraged the majority of their ambulations."[139]

The Comanches did not turn up on the South Plains as a unified body but rather in numerous family groups or bands. The band configuration of Comanche society was not rigid, and bands came together and broke apart depending on the needs and goals of their members. As many as thirteen different Comanche bands were identified during the historic period, and there were likely others that were never identified.[140]

COMANCHERIA

Having acquired horses in the first two decades of the eighteenth century, the Comanches migrated into Texas, usurping control of the region from the Apaches and Tonkawas. By 1725, most of the lands east of the Southern Rockies that had been called Apachería by the Spanish had become known as Comancheria. This Comanche sphere of influence consisted of all lands between the Spanish frontier and the Arkansas River lying between the Rocky Mountain Cordillera and the Cross Timbers of Texas. The heart of Comancheria covered six hundred miles from north to south and four hundred miles from east to west, lying entirely on the southern portion of the Great Plains from the ninety-eighth meridian to the foothills of the Rockies.[141]

The Penateka (Pen-ah-took-uhs) or "Honey Eater" band of Comanches occupied the Balcones Escarpment, the Upper Guadalupe River and the Verde Valley area. Their range extended from the Edwards Plateau to the headwaters of the central Texas rivers. Because of their site and situation, the Penatekas played the most legendary role in Texas history. "In legend and history, the Penatekas were the largest and most powerful of all Comanche bands. They had swept the Apaches into Mexico and fought the Spanish to a standstill in Texas."[142]

Comanche raids were legendary for the distance covered, striking hundreds of miles from their starting point. There were at least thirteen active bands of Comanches, with five playing prominent roles in Texas history. In the Kerr County area, the Penateka band of Comanches was virtually unchallenged. The Comanches' capacity to easily scamper across the rocky Hill Country allowed them to easily elude pursuers. So superior were the warriors that development west of the Balcones Escarpment came to a virtual halt. Fehrenbach, in his book on the Comanches, writes about the "Comanche barrier," noting, "By 1750, few, if any, surrounding peoples dared set foot in Comanche country."[143]

During 1779, the Comanches raided the Lipan Apache camps in the Verde Valley area northwest of San Antonio. The effect was to heighten the fears of the Spanish. In response, the citizens and militia from Béxar attacked a party of Comanches on the Guadalupe River. A number of Comanches were killed, and the Spaniards returned home with war trophies including bows and arrows, guns, an English hatchet, lances and a number of feathered war bonnets.[144]

Fearing that they would lose all of Texas to the Comanches, the Spanish negotiated a peace treaty with them in 1785. However, the Spanish did not make good on their pledges for trade goods and gifts. Consequently, the Comanches resumed their raiding of Spanish settlements. The Comanches rode into the Hill Country and the Kerr County area from the west all the way to the escarpment, massacring scattered bands of Tonkawas and Lipans wherever they were found. These fierce battles in the Guadalupe River Valley are unrecorded but must have been legendary events in the lives of these people.

Comanche Trail

Comanche presence in the Verde Valley is evidenced by the presence of the historical "Comanche Trail" that ran along what is now East Verde Creek Road in front of the present-day Camp Verde Store. This Comanche Trail or Trace is shown in the Camp Verde area on a map of Spanish Texas.[145] There were a number of Comanche Traces from north to south Texas, converging on Mexico. This particular Comanche Trail was mapped from Nacogdoches to the site of the present-day Camp Verde Store. Here it intersected the old Spanish Trail from San Antonio to the Presidio San Saba at present-day Menard.[146] If the Comanches went north from this intersection, they would arrive at the major camp in what is now Kerrville and then farther on the

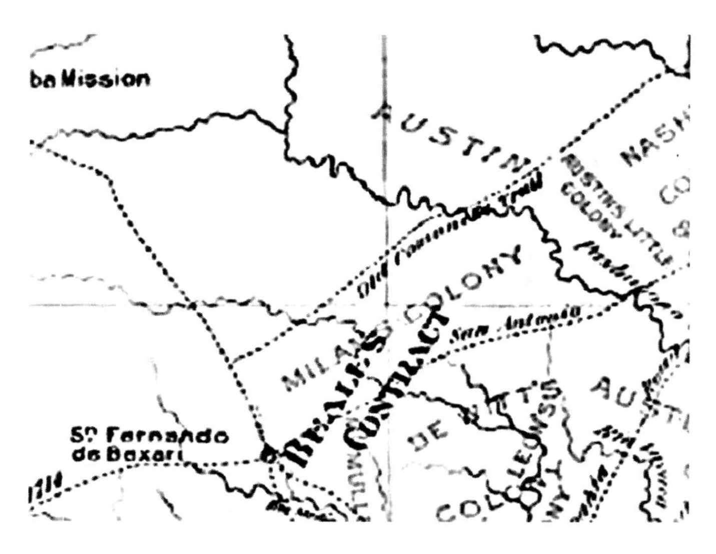

Map of the Comanche Trail. *Adapted from* Early Laws of Texas, *by Sayles, 1835.*

Edwards Plateau. Three miles north of Camp Verde, the Frio Trail followed Turtle Creek to its headwaters and then on to the headwaters of the south fork of the Guadalupe, where the route crossed the divide and descended into the Frio River canyons. The Comanches followed the trail south; they would transit Puerta de Bandera to access the trail to Las Moras Springs in present-day Kinney County. During the late eighteenth and early nineteenth centuries, the big spring was a stopping place on the eastern branch of the great Comanche Trail into Mexico.[147]

T.R. Fehrenbach describes this eastern Comanche Trace into Mexico: "A few miles north of the Rio Grande, near the present city of Del Rio, many trails of Comancheria converged into a broad roadway, beaten by the passage of thousands of unshod Amerindian ponies. This trail called the Comanche Trace was a distinctive landmark."[148]

By the 1820s, the Comanche hunting ranges extended from the Arkansas River to the Balcones Escarpment. The raiding range covered a vast area from Colorado to Durango in Mexico. They would raid over one thousand miles a year in search of scalps, horses and captives. Millions of dollars in property was looted or destroyed. Comanches are said to have killed more whites in proportion to their own numbers than any other Native American group.

Comanche Warrior

Warriors to the core, Comanches probably acquired their name from a Ute word meaning "anyone who wants to fight me all the time." Hunting and combat from horseback so engaged the Comanches that they seemed more at ease riding than on foot. The artist George Catlin observed, "In their movements they are heavy and ungraceful; and on their feet one of the most unattractive and slovenly races of Indians I have ever seen; but the moment they mount their horses, they seem at once metamorphosed, and surprise the spectator with the ease and grace of their movements." Mounted Comanche warriors were the most fearsome enemy ever faced by other Indians and Europeans alike in Texas.[149]

Much has been written about the savagery of the Comanches. The threat of a Comanche raid was so terrifying that their presence created a barrier to Anglo-American settlement west of the Balcones Escarpment. This was a clash of cultures, as the Comanches fought by their own customs, radically different from those of the Euro-Americans. What appeared as hideous atrocities to the settlers were cultural rituals to the Comanches. Fehrenbach writes:

> *The Anglo-Americans shared a common Indo-European cultural consciousness. This heritage included concepts of private property, hierarchy and aristocracy, moral dualism, and forms of serfdom, slavery, or other subordination. On the other hand, the "Amerindians" were isolated from all Europeans by world views and cultural divergences that had been widening for at least four thousand years. To become "civilized" like the Anglo-Americans (or Spaniards), the truly primitive tribesman had to do more than learn a new language or pick up a few new techniques. He had to betray his whole concept of the world and man's role in it. The Amerindian spirit world and the European universe of cause and effect did not just exist on higher and lower technical planes. They were utterly disparate and intimately hostile.*[150]

George Catlin painted the Comanches in the summer of 1834. With his artist's eye for detail, he noted their horsemanship: "He drew the reins upon a heavy Spanish bit, and every jump, plunged into the animal's sides, till they were a gore of blood, a huge pair of spurs."[151] The Comanches had learned from the Spanish the equestrian skills necessary to maintain and enhance their use of the horse. They replicated the Spanish saddles, bits, spurs, lassos, corrals, lances, herd management and decoration.[152]

On November 19, 1828, French naturalist Jean Louis Berlandier and Lieutenant Colonel José Francisco Ruiz departed San Antonio on a hunting and exploration expedition to the Hill Country.[153] They were escorted by thirty dragoons of the Alamo de Parras company[154] and traveled with a party of "fifty to eighty Comanches" led by Chiefs Quelluna (Keiuna) and El Ronco. Berlandier recorded the presence of a large camp of a Comanche chief at the location of present-day Kerrville.[155]

Berlandier, a member of the 1828 Mexican boundary and scientific expedition, observed that Comanches practiced a traditional custom when entering Bandera Pass:[156]

> *Here a Comanche warrior was buried, and since the natives often pass this way, every tribe that passes close enough to see the grave of one of their ancestors makes the customary offerings. On the grave they place arrows, bows, sundry weapons, enemy trophies, and the like, and even sacrifice mules and horses to his shade. The gorge, which is known for this custom, is strewn with the bones of the animals that have been sacrificed here. The grave itself is surrounded with skulls.*

Berlandier noted that the Comanche people, in particular, are very attentive to this custom: "Whenever they pass by the grave of a warrior they leave a few of their weapons. Women leave some fruit or a dish of something of which he was particularly fond."[157]

In the spring of 1836, the main thrust of early Euro-Texas settlement was up the south central river valleys of the Brazos, Colorado and Guadalupe. The Comanches fiercely resisted their encroachments with destructive and deadly raids on the frontier. Just above the Balcones Escarpment, where the Penateka Comanches liked to camp in the Hill Country canyons, the Texans and Comanches began to do battle.[158]

A cycle of raiding and retaliation on both sides climaxed during the presidency of Mirabeau B. Lamar. By July 25, 1839, the campaigns had destroyed or removed virtually all of the Native American population in the eastern half of Texas, opening up thousands of acres for settlement. The west was a different story. Despite campaigns by the Texas Rangers, the lands west of the Balcones Escarpment were in the control of the Penateka Comanches. Frontiersmen to the south and east of the Edwards Plateau continued to be in constant peril.[159]

Little Spaniard, a warrior. *By George Catlin, 1834. Courtesy of the Smithsonian Institution.*

The Comanches were a splendid and fearsome people. Billy Dixon, a buffalo hunter and frontier scout, described a Comanche charge at Adobe Walls:

> *There was never a more splendidly barbaric sight. In after years I was glad that I had seen it. Hundreds of warriors, the flower of the fighting men of the Southwestern Plains tribes, mounted upon their*

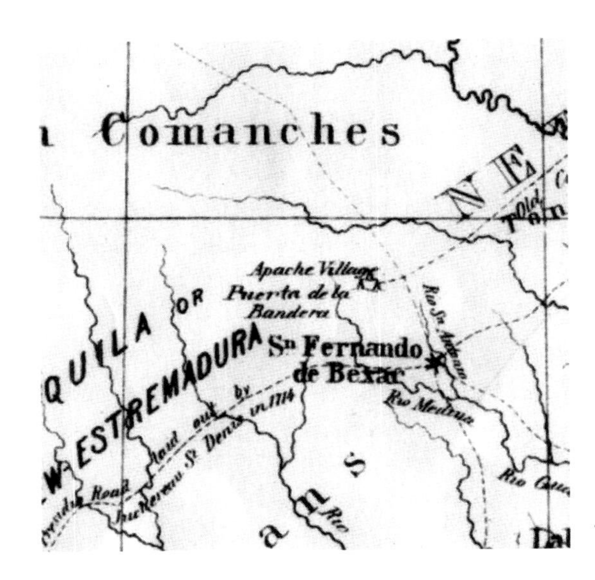

Map of Comancheria. *Adapted from Henderson K. Yokum,* 1805–1815 Map of Spanish Texas.

> *finest horses, armed with guns and lances, and carrying heavy shields of thick buffalo hide, were coming like the wind. Over all was splashed the rich colors of red, vermilion and ochre, on the bodies of men, on the bodies of running horses. Scalps dangled from bridles, gorgeous war-bonnets fluttered their plumes, bright feathers dangled from the tails and manes of the horses, and the bronzed, half-naked bodies of the riders glittered with ornaments of silver and brass. Behind this head-long charging host stretched the Plains, on whose horizon the rising sun was lifting its morning fires. The warriors seemed to emerge from this glorious background.*[160]

The Comanches adopted the Spanish use of bits and spurs, as well as a good copy of the Spanish saddle, which included a high pommel, saddle horn and cantle, along with stirrups. Comanche weapons included the bow and arrow, as well as the long lance, also adopted from the Spanish.[161]

A Comanche, riding at gallop, could loose twenty arrows, while a musket-armed soldier could only get off one shot and reload. Metal arrowheads became popular in the late seventeenth century. Low-grade iron arrow points turned out in quantity by forges were greatly sought after. A trading house could supply a packet of one dozen to the Indians at a cost of one medio real, one-sixteenth of a Spanish dollar, half a bit or six cents. Over two centuries, these iron arrowheads killed more human beings of both races than all the guns traded to the Indians combined.[162]

A local Euro-American captive of the Comanches, Clinton L. Smith, wrote about his life as a warrior. In his book, Smith writes:

> *They made their arrows out of dogwood switches, and made their bows out of wild mulberry and bois d'arc. In slipping around through the white settlements the Indians would pick up all of the hoop iron they could find and use this in making their arrow spikes. They also traded for this kind of iron from the Mexicans. Many people have asked if we used stone arrow spikes. We knew nothing about this kind of an arrowhead, for they belonged to tribes of a former age. The Mexicans also brought in iron or steel arrow spikes ready made, and all we had to do was fit them on a dogwood shaft and sharpen them.*[163]

Mirabeau B. Lamar abandoned Sam Houston's peace efforts, which he considered a failure, in favor of waging all-out war on the Comanche nation. Lamar's policy culminated in the Council House Fight in Béxar County. By invitation, thirty-three Penateka chiefs and warriors, accompanied by thirty-two other Comanches, arrived in San Antonio on March 19, 1840. Texas soldiers entered the Council House, where the peace talks were being held, and the commissioners informed the assembled chiefs that they were to be held as hostages until the remaining captives were released. In the ensuing mêlée, Texans attacked several Indians, while soldiers killed most of the Comanches who remained in the Council House courtyard. In the Council House Fight, thirty Penateka Comanche leaders and warriors, as well as some five women and children of the tribe, were killed by Texas troops in downtown San Antonio.[164]

Comanche hatred of Texans, who were regarded as treacherous, continued throughout the warfare era and contributed much to the violence of the frontier. In the summer of 1840, the Comanches swept down the Guadalupe valley, killing settlers, stealing horses and plundering and burning settlements. More than five hundred warriors led by Buffalo Hump, the celebrated war chief of the Penateka Comanches, raided the towns of Victoria and Linnville, killing twenty-five Texans.

After the Linnville raid of 1840, as the Comanches rode north, they were intercepted on August 12, 1840, at Plum Creek near the site of present-day Lockhart.[165] The Comanches were routed by a volunteer army under General Felix Huston, Colonel Edward Burleson and Captain Matthew Caldwell, as well as Texas Rangers under Ben McCulloch. Though some fifty Comanches were killed in the Battle of Plum Creek, the Texans continued to seek retribution. In October, Texas troops under the command of Colonel John H. Moore traveled three hundred miles up the Colorado River and destroyed a Comanche encampment near the site of present-day Colorado City.[166]

BUFFALO HUMP

Buffalo Hump was the war chief and representative of the largest and most famous band of the Comanches, the Penatekas. In 1844, Buffalo Hump met with Sam Houston and demanded that the white men stay off the Edwards Plateau, west of the Balcones Escarpment. In so doing, the Comanches were defining their frontier boundary as the Balcones Escarpment. President Houston tacitly agreed to this condition, and Texas Indian agents provided Buffalo Hump with gifts to demonstrate their goodwill. In spite of this, the Texas government was unable to hold back the surge of frontiersmen onto Comanche lands. Consequently, the Comanches resumed their raids. In response to these attacks, Texas Rangers assaulted Penateka encampments. Although Buffalo Hump managed to continue to fight for some time, in May 1846 he led the Comanche delegation at Council Springs and signed a treaty with the United States.[167]

On May 9, 1847, the Comanche chiefs, including Buffalo Hump, came to Fredericksburg to sign the Meusebach-Comanche Treaty. This treaty was one of the most important pioneer works of the Germans in Texas. John O. Meusebach and a delegation of German settlers met with the head chiefs—Buffalo Hump, Santa Anna and Mopechucope (Old Owl)—and their people. The treaty allowed Meusebach's settlers to go unharmed into Comanche territory and the Comanches to go to the white settlements; promised mutual reports on wrongdoing; and provided for survey of lands in the San Saba area with a payment of at least $1,000 to the Indians. The treaty opened more than three million acres of land to settlement.[168] It is believed to be the only Texas treaty made with the Indians that was not broken by either side. An annual powwow celebration is held in Fredericksburg in honor of this unbroken treaty.[169]

Ferdinand Roemer, a noted German scientist who was traveling in America at the time of the meetings in the mid- and late 1840s, attended the Fredericksburg council between the chiefs and white representatives. Roemer characterizes Buffalo Hump vividly as

> *the pure unadulterated picture of a North American Indian, who, unlike the rest of his tribe, scorned every form of European dress. His body naked, a buffalo robe around his loins, brass rings on his arms, a string of beads around his neck, and with his long, coarse black hair hanging down, he sat there with the serious facial expression of the North American Indian which seems to be apathetic to the European. He attracted our special attention because he had distinguished himself through great daring and bravery in expeditions against the Texas frontier, which he had engaged in times past.*

In 1855, a reservation was established on the Clear Fork of the Brazos River, and by 1857, more than four hundred Comanches were collected there. They were later removed to tracts in the Indian Territory (Oklahoma) and in the Texas panhandle. Other Comanches continued the time-honored tradition of raiding deep into the mountains of Mexico.

The 1867 Treaty of Medicine Lodge Creek, the last treaty made with the Comanches, established a reservation for the Comanches, Kiowas and Kiowa Apaches in southwestern Indian Territory between the Washita and Red Rivers. The treaty did not greatly improve conditions in Texas, however, because the Comanches would not stay on the lands allotted them and continued to conduct destructive raids in Texas.[170] In the spring of 1869, the Kiowas and Comanches swarmed out of Indian Territory, leaving terror in their wake. Raiding escalated through the autumn, and the Kiowas sent emissaries to urge the Cheyennes to full war. Texas was ablaze.[171]

Sporadic raids by both Lipan Apaches and Penateka Comanches continued in the Kerr County area through the 1870s. An Indian raiding party at Kerrville attacked Dominic Michon, an emigrant from France, in 1874. The same day, these Indians then attacked and wounded George P. Phillips. Both men escaped.[172] In 1877, a band of thirty Indians passed near Kerrville on a horse-stealing raid. This raiding party killed Sam Spears.[173] The pioneer family of Susan and James Dowdy moved from Goliad to Kerr County in 1878 and settled on Johnson Creek. Shortly after the family arrived, Indians killed four of the Dowdy children—Alice, Martha, Susan and James—while they were tending sheep near their home. The attack occurred on October 5, 1878, at a site about three and a half miles northwest of present Ingram. The victims were buried the following day at Sunset Cemetery, northwest of Ingram. This incident was one of the last Indian raids in Kerr County.[174]

Kiowas

The Kiowas formed an alliance with the Comanches around 1790, joining with them in raiding expeditions. This tribe apparently originated in the area of modern-day Yellowstone Park but migrated south after the introduction of the horse culture. They became among the greatest horsemen in the world and, along with the Comanches, the most feared of the Plains tribes. The Kiowa chief Santanta (White Bear) led his people in the titanic struggle to expel the white man from his ancestral homeland. One of the most feared of all Indian leaders, Santanta's life inspired the character of Blue Duck in Larry McMurtry's classic Texas novel *Lonesome Dove*: "Santanta would ride into Fort Chadbourne splendidly mounted, dressed in beautiful fashion carrying a shield ornamented with a white woman's scalp from which hung a suite of beautiful brown hair."[175]

Gaining horses, slaves and guns from the Spanish, the Kiowas evolved into completely nomadic life ways of predation, pillage and warfare until they became one of the most feared and hated of the Plains tribes. Constantly, they kept the greatest numbers of horses of all the Plains Indians. The Kiowas traded with the Comanches. Trade items included guns, ammunition, metal arrowheads, horses and captives. These items came from the east by way of the Wichitas and Taovayas, who traded with the French and English.[176]

Santanta, Kiowa chief. *Photographed by William S. Soule, 1869–74.*

Kiowa presence in the Hill Country and the Balcones Canyonlands waned in the succeeding decades. After 1860, the Kiowas rarely ventured into the region, remaining to the north in the lands for which they are better known. Notable exceptions occurred in 1860, 1872 and 1873. In 1860, a member of a Kiowa band on its way to raid in Mexico was killed while attempting to steal horses near the Pecos River. Then, in 1872, a Kiowa/Comanche raiding party attacked a government wagon train at Howard Wells near the Devil's

River, and another Kiowa/Comanche band traveled to Mexico below Eagle Pass. On their return via the Devil's River, they encountered an army scouting party that killed two of their members. This battle may be immortalized in the rock art at 41VV327, a site located on a tributary of the Devil's River.[177]

By June 1875, the tribe was forced onto the Fort Sill reservation in Oklahoma.[178]

6

Estados Unidos Mexicanos

Spanish Texas was a province of New Spain from 1690 until 1821. On August 24, 1821, Juan O'Donoju met Agustín de Iturbide in Córdoba and signed a treaty granting Mexico independence from Spain. The treaty ended the Mexican War of Independence.

The failure of Spain, and later Mexico, to populate the Central Texas region is understandable considering the rugged remoteness of the region and the long distances to supply centers. By the year 1821, when the granting of land for Moses Austin's colony opened the gate for immigration from the United States, there were still no significant settlements north of San Antonio.[179]

Department of Béxar

Soon after the first Euro-American colonists came to Texas in 1821, San Antonio became the western outpost of settlement. The Verde Valley was situated in Coahuila y Tejas, one of the constituent states of the newly established Estados Unidos de Mexicanos. The new state of Coahuila y Tejas had two capitals: first Saltillo and then Monclova. For administrative purposes, the state of Coahuila y Tejas was divided into three districts: Béxar, comprising the area covered by Texas; Monclova, comprising northern Coahuila; and Río Grande Saltillo, comprising southern Coahuila. The Béxar district administered the Verde Valley until the Texas Revolution.[180]

When Mexico won independence from Spain, and in the summer of 1821, at Béxar, Tejanos and Anglos swore allegiance to the new nation.[181] Mexico continued the Spanish colonization plan after its independence in 1821 by granting contracts to impresarios who would settle and supervise selected, qualified immigrants. During the late 1820s and early 1830s, increasing numbers of Euro-American settlers began moving to San Antonio, though the city remained predominately Mexican at the beginning of the Texas Revolution. There were no Mexican land grants along Verde Creek.

The Constitución Federal de los Estados Unidos Mexicanos de 1824 was enacted on October 4, 1824. In the new constitution, the republic took the name of United Mexican States and was defined as a representative federal republic, with Catholicism as the official and unique religion, all others being prohibited. As early as 1824, Miguel Ramos Arispe, author of the (Mexican) constitution of 1824, referred to the citizens of Texas as Tejano in correspondence with the town council of Béxar. After the Mexican War of Independence and the establishment of a federal government, the term "Coahuiltejano" denoted the citizens of the Mexican state of Coahuila and Texas.[182]

Tejanos

"Tejano society was a composite of many cultures and races, which produced a complex mestizaje, Tlascalan and native Texan Indian, Spanish and European," writes Andres Tijerina in his book on Tejanos and Texas. He notes that the "defensive and presidial nature of the frontera (frontier) tended to unify Tejanos socially as well as militarily, with the presidio as the integral institution in this unity."[183]

Mexican presidial soldier. *By Lino Sanchez y Tapia, 1828.*

The Mexican army assigned troops to the presidios of the Texas frontera. By 1826, the Béxar garrison was completely reorganized. The government began to enlist local Bexareños[184] into the Mexicano Presidial, causing a statistical decline in the population census because of their new, special status. In addition to the presidial soldiers, there were also armed citizens, Ciudadanos Armados, defending the frontera. They served in military forays, many of which were into Apachería and Comancheria, as Mexican rancheros began to settle lands north and west of San Antonio.[185]

ALAMO DE PARRAS

La Segunda Compañía Volante de San Carlos de Parras (Alamo de Parras), commanded by Ruiz, was a company of one hundred Spanish colonial mounted lancers, who had arrived in early 1803 to strengthen the existing San Antonio garrison. In the early 1800s, expansionists, like Aaron Burr, called for the invasion of Spanish territory, prompting Spain to look toward the United States with great anxiety. To repel any possible foreign invasion, Spanish troops were concentrated on the Texas frontier. As the first of several reinforcement efforts, the Alamo de Parras Company marched under orders from Chihuahua to Texas to San Antonio de Béjar (Béxar). Most of the soldiers arrived on the Rio San Antonio by January 1803, with their families following that spring.[186]

This company would remain at San Antonio for the next thirty-two years, assimilating into the existing community and becoming involved in San Antonio's military, civil and political affairs, including the Mexican War for Independence and the Texas Revolution. Their lasting legacy would be to give their name to the former Mission San Antonio de Valero that would become known as the Alamo because of their association.[187]

JOSÉ FRANCISCO RUIZ

José Francisco Ruiz is the iconic frontiersman of northern Mexico. Beginning a long military career, Ruiz joined the Béxar Provincial Militia on January 14, 1811, with the rank of lieutenant. He joined the Republican Army at Béxar and served first under José Bernardo Gutierrez de Lara and then José Alvarez de Toledo y Dubois. Ruiz was promoted in 1823 to army captain, unassigned, with the rank of lieutenant colonel. His commission was confirmed on September 23, 1825.[188]

In 1828, Ruiz returned to Béxar, where he commanded the Alamo de Parras.[189] In the fall of 1828, Ruiz led the group of Mexican soldiers and boundary commission members, including naturalist Jean-Louis Berlandier, on a bear and buffalo hunt into the Hill Country northwest of San Antonio with the cooperation of local Comanche leaders Reyuna and El Ronca. On this expedition, this group visited the Comanche camp at today's Kerrville and the old Lipan camp at the headwaters of the Guadalupe, Ojo de Agua de Guadalupe.[190] Berlandier noted the Labor de los Lipanes, the Lipans' Field, near the headwaters. Berlandier was part of the Mexican Boundary Commission and compiled authoritative information on over forty Native American tribes in the territory surrounding San Antonio.

From November 19 to December 18, Ruiz and a military party explored the Los Almagres silver mines on the San Saba River. It was probably during this time that Ruiz wrote his "Report on the Indian Tribes of Texas in 1818," preserved in the Rare Book and Manuscript Library at Yale University.[191] During his years in the military, Ruiz gained the trust of the Indians as negotiator. The Shawnees referred to him as "a good man no lie and a friend of the Indians."[192]

For a while, the Mexican and Comanche border trade flourished between San Antonio and Nacogdoches. Berlandier reported how eastern Comanches visited the Nacogdoches presidio "in caravans of several hundred, provided they are at peace with the garrison, to sell their buffalo hides (covered with painting), smoked and dried meat, and, above all, furs."[193] This route was the basis of the historic Comanche Trail from Nacogdoches to Camp Verde.

Settlement Patterns

After the Mexican Revolution, the population of Béxar and the surrounding region fell markedly and did not begin to grow again until the end of the decade. Population began to creep westward up the Guadalupe River, much to the ire of the Comanches living there.

By 1835, Antonio López de Santa Anna had established himself as a dictator in Mexico. Among Euro-American colonists and Tejanos alike, the call for Texas independence grew louder. In the fall of 1835, many Texans concluded that liberalism and republicanism in Mexico, as reflected in its constitution of 1824, were dead. On March 2, 1836, a delegation at Washington-on-the-Brazos adopted the Texas Declaration of Independence, and thus was created the Republic of Texas. Santa Anna brought his army to Texas to put down the rebellion, and events followed in quick succession.[194]

7
Republic of Texas

The Texas Revolution began with the Battle of Gonzales in October 1835 and ended with the Battle of San Jacinto on April 21, 1836. During the Texas Revolution, San Antonio was the site of several battles, including the siege of Béxar and the Battle of the Alamo, which made San Antonio one of the most fought-over cities in North America.[195] After the evacuation of Mexican forces, the Republic of Texas organized Béxar County in December 1836.

Béxar County

The newly formed Béxar County, which included what is now Kerr County, covered much of the western edge of settlement in Texas. During the late Mexican period, Texas had been divided into four departments, with the Department of Béxar stretching from the Rio Grande to the panhandle and as far west as El Paso. With the winning of Texas independence, the departments became counties, and on December 20, 1836, Béxar County was established, with San Antonio as county seat.

As early as the spring of 1836, settlements began expanding up the valley of the Guadalupe River. The Penateka Comanches reacted with terrifying and deadly raids on the frontier. The area around Kerr County was apparently prized by the Comanches because of the Hill Country canyons, streams and game.

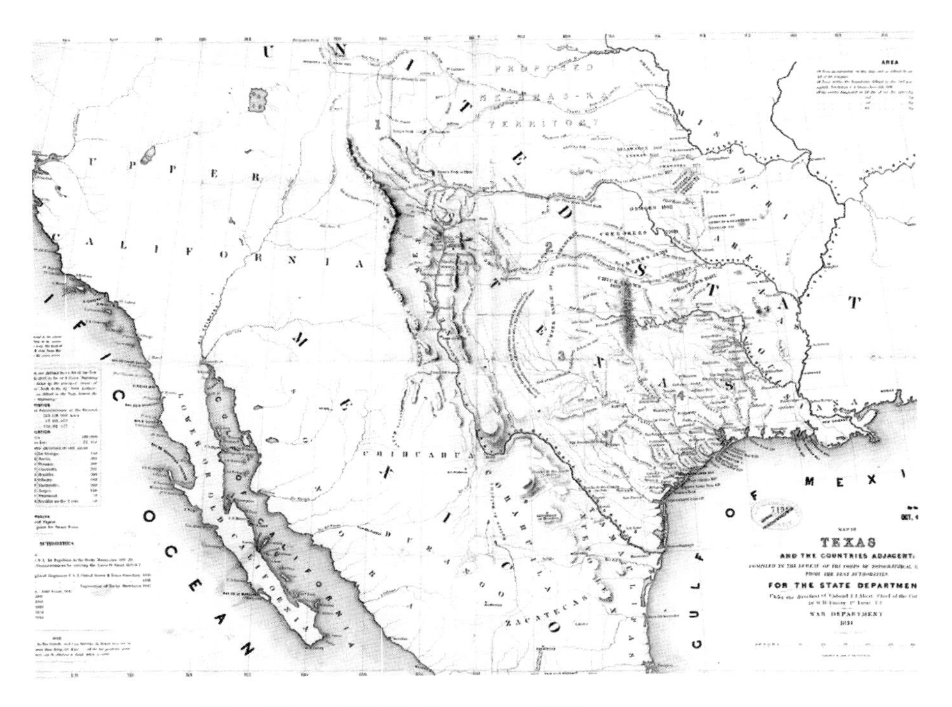

Map of the Republic of Texas. *U.S. War Department, 1844.*

The Verde Valley became the frontier once again, with settlers moving up the Guadalupe and Medina Rivers. Comanches and Apaches fought to keep these settlements off the Balcones Escarpment. On December 1, 1838, the Congress of the Republic of Texas enacted a law authorizing a regiment of 840 mounted men for the protection of the frontier. By December, the Texas Congress had made provisions to add 472 more men. In January 1839, Congress enacted another law, adding 112 additional rangers. This was the beginning of the legendary ranger forces in Texas. Camp Verde was part of their dominion.[196]

ADELSVEREIN

Foremost among the early settlers appearing in the Verde Creek–Guadalupe River area was the Adelsverein, also known as the Mainzer Verein, the Texas-Verein and the German Emigration Company. It was officially named the

Adelsverein. *Logo of Verein zum Schutze Deutscher Einwanderer in Texas.*

Verein zum Schutze deutscher Einwanderer in Texas (Society for the Protection of German Immigrants in Texas). Provisionally organized on April 20, 1842, by twenty-one German noblemen at Biebrich on the Rhine, near Mainz, the society represented a significant effort to establish a new Germany on Texas soil by means of an organized mass emigration.[197]

The first Adelsverein immigrants disembarked in Texas in December 1844, near Carlshafen (later Indianola), the society's port of entry established by Prince Carl of Solms-Braunfels. On May 8, 1845, John O. Meusebach, Solms's successor as general commissioner in Texas, arrived at Carlshafen; in November, he began preparing for the arrival of 4,000 new immigrants. Fredericksburg, the society's second colony, was established by Meusebach in 1846 near the Pedernales River, where the year before he had bought over eleven thousand acres of head right land. Between October 1845 and April 1846, 5,257 German emigrants were brought to Texas. In 1847, five settlements—Bettina, Castell, Leiningen, Meerholz and Schoenburg—were established in the Fisher-Miller grant on the banks of the Llano River. John O. Meusebach also owned land on Verde Creek near Camp Verde.[198]

War with Mexico

The United States became alarmed over the policy of Great Britain toward Texas. The British were opposed to annexation and even contemplated the use of force to prevent it. Annexation of the Republic of Texas became an issue in the presidential election of 1844; James K. Polk, who favored annexation, was elected. Tyler, feeling the need of haste if British designs were to be circumvented, suggested that annexation be accomplished by a joint resolution offering Texas statehood on certain conditions, the acceptance of which by Texas would complete the merger. The United States Congress passed the annexation resolution on February 28, 1845.[199]

In May 1845, the United States dispatched a fleet of warships to protect the Texas coast. Hostilities with Mexico and the Indians reached a settlement. Texas was admitted as a state on December 29, 1845. The Republic of Texas, after nine years, eleven months and seventeen days, was no more. Texas was annexed as a slave state rather than as a territory. It kept its public lands and paid its own public debts. It retained the power to divide itself into as many as four additional states.

Many Texans—in all, some five to seven thousand men—volunteered during the summer of 1846 for service in the U.S. Army as it prepared to invade Mexico. Texas soldiers played key roles in General Zachary Taylor's army as it took control of northern Mexico by defeating Mexican forces at Monterrey in September 1846 and holding its own against vastly superior numbers at Buena Vista in February 1847. Captain Ben McCulloch's company of rangers served so effectively as scouts and spies that Taylor attached them to his headquarters rather than to Henderson's command.[200]

The rangers under John Coffee Hays's leadership fought brilliantly, although their appearance and behavior often appalled officers in the regular army. "A more reckless, devil-may-care looking set, it would be impossible to find this side of the Infernal Regions," one cavalryman wrote. "Take them altogether, with their uncouth costumes, bearded faces, lean and brawny forms, fierce wild eyes and swaggering manners; they were fit representatives of the outlaws which made up the population of the Lone Star State." Indeed, the rangers were almost too rough and ready for "Old Rough and Ready," General Taylor himself. "Them Texas troops are the damndest troops in the world," he reportedly said. "We can't do without them in a fight, and we can't do anything with them out of a fight." Later, in 1847, Hays formed another ranger unit and joined the army commanded by General Winfield Scott that landed at Veracruz and moved inland to occupy Mexico City and end the war. Hays's rangers kept communications and supply lines open for Scott's army and in the process meted out such ruthless and deadly treatment to Mexican guerrillas that the civilian population referred to them as "los Tejanos diablos."[201]

Shingle Makers

Drawn by giant cypress trees, settlers began moving into the Verde Creek area and the upper Guadalupe River. The bald cypress (*Taxodium distichum*) is a member of the Redwood family and can grow to a height of up to 120 feet. Most live up to 600 years, but some individual cypress trees have survived 1,200 years. In 1846, Ferdinand Roemer reported cypress trees on the Guadalupe River with a diameter of 10 feet.[202] Regarding the cypress trees, J. Frank Dobie wrote about "Ingram's Snag," with a hollow "ample enough to camp in."[203] At this time, the shingles were wrought by hand, using large two-man saws, axes, wedges, sledgehammers, froes and carving bench vises.

The most well-known shingle maker on the upper Guadalupe River was Joshua D. Brown, who is celebrated for establishing what is now Kerrville. Brown, drawn by tales of giant cypress trees, ventured upriver from Curry's Creek in 1848 with a party of ten men. At the site of Kerrville, Brown found an abundance of giant cypress trees with diameters of eight to ten feet. There were other nameless shingle makers working the cypress trees along the rivers and creeks of the area at this time.

Unknown to Joshua Brown was the fact that Robert Neighbors, the federal Indian agent, was busy relocating the Lipan Apaches to the upper Guadalupe River in 1848. Brown and his crew were soon driven away by Comanches and Lipan Apaches and retreated downriver to safer locations.

Settlers continued to move up the Guadalupe River. Fredericksburg was settled in 1846, Curry's Creek in 1847, Sisterdale in 1848, Boerne in 1849 and Comfort in 1854. In 1852, Brown returned and purchased the land on which the city of Kerrville is now located. His shingle camp was located on Spring Creek—now known as Spring Street along Water Street in Kerrville. Many other settlers soon followed.[204]

By 1856, a number of families were living in old Zanzenberg, today's Center Point, at the confluence of Verde Creek and the Guadalupe River. Kerrville consisted of only a few cabins and shingle makers' camps.[205]

Kerr County was organized on January 25, 1856, out of Bexar County and included portions of today's Real and Kendall Counties.[206] When formed, Kerr County contained many land grants issued by the Republic of Texas. A great deal of the lands along the Guadalupe River had been surveyed and granted by the republic between 1838 and 1840. There were never any Spanish or Mexican land grants in the area of this county.[207]

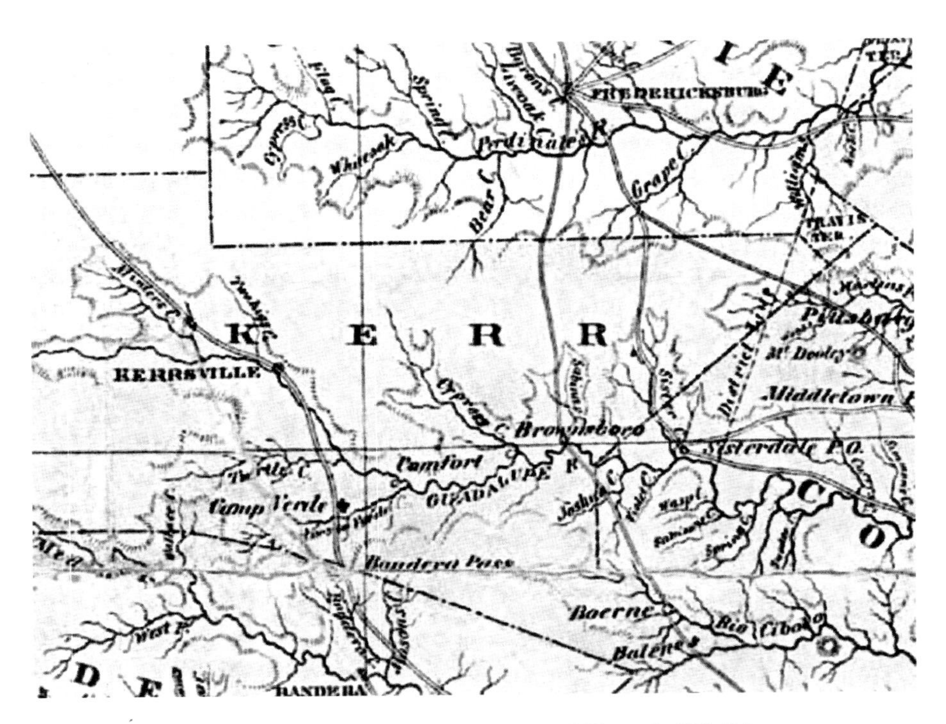

Map of Kerr County, 1856. *Adapted from* Map of State of Texas, *by J.H. Colton.*

Indian raids continued even as Kerr County was being established. Six men "were killed and scalped by Indians in Kerr County" in late November 1856. The San Antonio, Texas newspaper reported that "seven persons had encamped for the night, and the Indians came upon them while asleep, killed and scalped four, and left two mortally wounded; one only can survive of the seven."[208]

8

Texas Rangers

In 1823, only two years after Euro-American colonization formally began in Texas, empresario Stephen F. Austin hired ten experienced frontiersmen as rangers for a punitive expedition against a band of Indians. However, not until 1835 did Texas lawmakers institute a specific force known as the Texas Rangers.[209]

The Republic of Texas could not afford a sizable permanent army. Frontier militias were of little use. Euro-Americans brought farm horses to Texas. Any fine racing breeds were too delicate for the rough Hill Country. The weapons of the Anglo-Americans were inadequate for the task of frontier defense. The Kentucky rifle was unsuited for cavalry warfare; it was long and heavy with a short stock. Although extremely accurate while at rest, it was useless from horseback. As Fehrenbach notes, "In the time it took a frontiersman to get off two shots with his clumsy muzzle-loader, a mounted Comanche could cross three hundred yards and loose a score of shafts." When the Euro-American had made his one shot, he was left with a knife or tomahawk for close fighting. The Comanche would charge with a long lance and kill the frontiersman without fighting hand-to-hand.[210]

The organization had a complement of fifty-six men in three companies, each officered by a captain and two lieutenants, whose immediate superior and leader had the rank of major and was subject to the commander in chief of the regular army. The major was responsible for enlisting recruits, enforcing rules and applying discipline. Officers received the same pay as

United States dragoons and privates: $1.25 a day. However, they supplied their own mounts, equipment, arms and rations. At all times, they had to be ready to ride, equipped "with a good and sufficient horse...[and] with one hundred rounds of powder and ball."

A new breed of horse was developed to compete with the Comanche. The new stock was developed from Spanish mustangs mixed with Kentucky and Arabian strains: mounts larger, heavier and longer winded than the Amerindian ponies.[211]

James W. Nichols, in his journal, describes the routine training sessions for rangers near Seguin in Captain Jack Hays's company in 1843:

> *We put up a post about the size of a common man, then put up another about 40 yards farther on. We would run our horses full speed and discharge our rifles at the first post, draw our pistles and fire at the second. At first thare was some wild shooting but we had not practised two months until thare was not many men that would not put his balls in the center of the posts. Then we drew a ring about the size of a mans head and soon every man could put both his balls in the circul. We would practics this awhile, then try rideing like the Comanche Indians. After practisng for three or four months we became so purfect that we would ran our horses half or full speede and pick up a hat, a coat, a blanket, or rope, or even a silver dollar, stand up in the saddle, throw ourselves on the side of our horses with only a foot and a hand to be seen, and shoot our pistols under the horses neck, rise up and reverse, etc.*[212]

The Texas Rangers would play a significant role in the history of Camp Verde and the Texas Hill Country. Among the famous Texas Rangers who operated in the Texas Hill Country at this time were Captain John Coffee Hays, Chief Flacco, Captain John W. Sansom, Captain Big Foot Wallace, Captain John S. (Rip) Ford and Captain Charles S. de Montel.

JOHN COFFEE HAYS

John (Jack) Coffee Hays came to Texas after the Mexican surrender at San Jacinto on April 21, 1836, but he still joined the Army of the Republic commanded by General Thomas J. Rusk. Hays officially became a Texas Ranger in December 1836. He enlisted for twelve months with pay of thirty

John Coffee Hays. *Courtesy of the Texas Ranger Hall of Fame and Museum.*

dollars per month. Also included were provisions for himself and his horse. However, he had to provide his own horse, rifle, pistols and other equipment, which were subject to inspection.[213]

In 1840, Hays was appointed a captain of the rangers. He proved himself a fearless fighter and a good leader of men. His ranger companies, often mixed groups of Anglos, Tejanos and Indians, engaged in battles and skirmishes with the Comanches and other hostile Indian tribes throughout the early years of the 1840s. Hays and his rangers were involved in important actions at Plum Creek, Cañon de Ugalde, Bandera Pass, Painted Rock, Salado and Walker's Creek. The battle at Walker's Creek marked a turning point in Indian warfare with the first effective use of repeating handguns in close combat with the Comanches.

John Coffee Hays commanded the San Antonio station, "the most dangerous and important Ranger post in western Texas." He personally trained ranger captains Ben McCulloch and Sam Walker. In a decisive action, Hays introduced the new five-shot Colt revolver (Paterson model) into the Comanche war. Hays's tactics with the repeating pistols so distressed the Penatekas that they soon sought a treaty. For the Comanches, the fighting against the Tejanos had ceased to be a sport.[214]

Battle of Walker's Creek

On June 9, 1844, Captain Hays and his rangers were attacked by a Comanche war party led by Yellow Wolf, which had recently been raiding into Béxar County. Noah Cheery called out, "Jerusalem, captain, yonder comes a thousand Indians!"[215]

The rangers quickly saddled and mounted, while the Comanches, whose numbers were variously estimated at from forty to upwards of two hundred warriors, fell back into a thicket from which they apparently hoped to spring an ambush. From behind rocks and trees, they taunted the rangers in Spanish, hoping to provoke a frontal assault. Hays, however, led his men around the hill, his movement shielded by the ravine, and attacked the Indian line from the rear. The fight for the hilltop, wrote Ben McCulloch, was soon hand-to-hand, and "they took it rough and tumble." The rangers repulsed two counterattacks on their flanks, after which the Indians fled the field and were pursued for three miles under heavy fire from the rangers' revolvers. "Crowd them! Powder-burn them!" were Hays's orders.[216]

This battle took place at the Pinta Crossing of the Guadalupe River, near its confluence with West Sister Creek, in the area of present Kendall County (29°57.529′N, 93°42.925′W). It became famous as the Battle of Walker's Creek.[217] Ranger losses amounted to one killed and four seriously wounded.[218]

Jack Hays's rangers were the first to be equipped with the new, five-shot revolving pistol manufactured by Colonel Sam Colt in 1844. The rangers quickly became legendary as one of the most brutally efficient tracking and killing machines ever fielded.[219] For all their delicacy, the Paterson Colts provided unprecedented firepower. A ranger armed with a Paterson and an extra cylinder could fire ten rounds in forty seconds, and Hays's rangers frequently carried two pistols and spare cylinders. At last, they had

Battle of Walker's Creek. *Courtesy of the Texas Ranger Hall of Fame and Museum.*

the firepower to stand up to Comanches in mounted combat and more than match their rapidity of fire with bow and arrow.[220]

The Battle of Walker's Creek was a defining moment in the battle between the Indians and the Texas Rangers. After this fight, combat would never be the same. The Paterson revolver changed everything, and the pendulum swung in favor of the rangers. The Walker's Creek fight is depicted on the cylinder of the 1847 Walker Dragoon model Colt revolver, designed by Texas Ranger Sam Walker.[221]

Battle of Bandera Pass

On the southern edge of the Verde Valley, three miles from Camp Verde, Captain John Coffee Hays is said to have been involved in the legendary Battle of Bandera Pass in June 1842.[222] The date, as well as the actual event, is in dispute.[223] No apparent primary source documents this fight. The story seems to be based on A.J. Sowell's account of the battle that was then published in the *Frontier Times*, becoming a significant part of Texas Ranger mythology.[224]

According to Sowell's account, Hays and his rangers sortied from San Antonio to the head of the Guadalupe River. Included in this scouting party were a number of celebrated Indian fighters: Ben Highsmith, Creed Taylor, Sam Walker, Robert Addison Gillespie, P.H. Bell, Kit Ackland, Sam Luckey, James Dunn, Tom Galberth, George Neill and Frank Chevallier.[225]

As the story goes, when the rangers were a third of the way through the pass, the first warning of the presence of danger came; the Comanche "war whoop" echoed through the canyon. Hundreds of Comanches charged on horseback into the battle. The Comanches smacked the rangers' horses with their shields, panicking the mounts. The horses plunged and reared, wounded and scared. Several rangers fell, killed or wounded. The rangers were surrounded and beleaguered. Nevertheless, the mêlée was controlled when Hays, cool and collected, yelled out above the tumult, "Steady there boys…dismount and tie those horses, we can whip them…No doubt about that." The fighting was vicious and hand-to-hand.[226]

According to A.J. Sowell, nearly a third of the rangers were killed or wounded, five killed and six wounded. Withdrawing to the springs at the south end of the pass, the rangers tended the wounded, among them Sam Luckey, Kit Ackland, James Dunn, Ben Highsmith and Tom Galberth. The five dead rangers were buried there at the south end of Bandera Pass. The Comanches buried their dead at the north end of the pass in the Verde Valley.[227]

CONTROVERSY

There is some controversy as to the authenticity of reports of the Battle of Walker's Creek and the Battle of Bandera Pass, both featuring Captain Hays and his rangers. Jack Hays is a mythic hero for his fight with the Comanches in Bandera Pass. This battle is a major part of the Verde Creek story. There is some difference of opinion regarding the veracity of the Bandera Pass fight.[228]

Numerous publications ranging from pulp fiction to scholarly works describe this battle in detail. Critics of this history are reporting that the Battle of Bandera Pass was, in fact, the Battle of Walker's Creek. Other critics such as Mike Cox, in his book *Wearing the Cinco Peso: 1821–1900*, contends that perhaps neither fight occurred.[229]

COLONEL FLACCO

Captain Hays had a good working relationship with the Lipan Apaches in and around the Kerr County area. Flacco the Elder and Flacco the Younger, Lipan Apache chiefs, were both friends of the Texas settlers and were frequently used as scouts and guides against the Comanche Indians and the Mexicans. The Lipan war chief, named Flacco the Younger, became a close associate of Hays. The two rode together on many expeditions. Flacco became Hays's teacher in Indian customs and practices.[230]

In gratitude for his service to Texas, Flacco was awarded the title of colonel. With the rank came the uniform of a full colonel, including the plumed hat and fancy sword.[231]

Hays described the chief as "tall and erect, with well-shaped limbs. He gave an impression of bounding elasticity. His circlet of eagle feathers was set back on his forehead so that it revealed his black eyes and gave to his bearing a fierce alertness coupled with strength and agility. Flacco's general appearance was suggestive of the hawk and the panther." Hays also credited Flacco with saving his life on several occasions in battles against the Comanches. Flacco the Younger was murdered west of San Antonio. Although Sam Houston and other Texas government officials tried to blame the murder on Mexican bandits or Cherokees, Chief Flacco was convinced that his son had been killed by Anglo settlers.[232]

John W. Sansom

John W. Sansom played a key role in the defense of the frontier at Camp Verde. A frontier militia officer and Unionist leader, Sansom grew to manhood at Curry's Creek settlement, in the area of present-day Kendall County, where his family engaged in farming and ranching. In 1855, he became a private in the local company of Texas Rangers, thus beginning nearly thirty years of public service. That year, he took part in the Callahan expedition. By 1856, he was a captain.[233]

During the Civil War, Sansom, from a staunch Unionist family, was invited to accept a position of leadership in the Union Loyal League, a militia organized to protect parts of Kendall, Gillespie and Kerr Counties from Indian raids and Confederate actions. After the Battle of the Nueces on August 10, 1862, of which Sansom wrote the authoritative account, *Battle of Nueces River in Kinney County, Tex., Aug. 10, 1862*,[234] the league was forced underground, and Sansom, along with many other Texas Unionists like Andrew J. Hamilton and Edmund J. Davis, went to New Orleans after that city was taken by Union forces. Sansom joined the First Texas Cavalry, USA, and took part in the Rio Grande campaign.[235]

After the war, Sansom continued his service as a captain and later major of ranger troops in the Hill Country. One episode during this time was the capture by the Indians of Sansom's young cousins, Clint and Jeff Smith. In 1882, New Mexico invited Sansom to help organize the territorial troops of that state. In 1883, he retired to ranch holdings he had acquired earlier in Uvalde County, Texas. In 1904, he and his family retired completely from public and business life and moved to a home at 1102 North Flores Street in San Antonio. Sansom married Helen Victoria Patton in Blanco County in 1860. They had one child, a daughter named Elizabeth. Preceded in death by his wife, Sansom died on June 19, 1920, in San Antonio and was buried in the Mission Burial Park, near San José Mission, in San Antonio.[236]

Big Foot Wallace

Big Foot Wallace. *Courtesy of the Texas Ranger Hall of Fame and Museum.*

William Alexander Anderson (Big Foot) Wallace, soldier and Texas Ranger, was a magnificent physical specimen. In his prime, he stood six feet, two inches "in his moccasins" and weighed 240 pounds without surplus fat. He was with the Texans who fought General Adrián Woll's invading Mexican army near San Antonio in 1842 and then volunteered for the Somervell and Mier expeditions. Some of his most graphic memories were of his experiences in Perote Prison. As soon as he was released, he joined the Texas Rangers under John Coffee (Jack) Hays and was with the rangers in the Mexican War. In the 1850s, Wallace commanded, as captain, a ranger company of his own, fighting border bandits as well as Indians. During the Civil War, he helped guard the frontier against the Comanche Indians. At one time, Wallace had a little ranch on the Medina River on land granted him by the State of Texas.[237]

His knife was named "Old Butcher" and his rifle was called "Sweet Lips." He described himself, saying, "You see, boys, I am a pretty stout man yet, but in those days, without meaning to brag, I do not believe there was a white man west of the Colorado River that could stand up against me in a regular catamount, bear hug, or hand-to-hand fight."[238]

John S. (Rip) Ford

John Salmon Ford moved to Texas in June 1836 and served in the Texas army until 1838, rising to the rank of first lieutenant under John Coffee (Jack) Hays. During the Mexican War, Ford was adjutant of Hays's regiment and in command of a spy company. While serving as adjutant, Ford acquired the lasting nickname "Rip." When officially sending out notices of deaths, he kindly included at the beginning of the message the words "Rest in Peace"; later, under the exigencies of battle conditions, this message was shortened to "RIP."[239]

In January 1858, Governor Runnels appointed John S. (Rip) Ford to take command of all state troops and attack the Indian raiders. Ford's force of slightly more than 100 rangers, supported by 110 Indians from the Brazos Reservation who wanted to prove their loyalty, crossed the Red River into present-day Oklahoma and attacked the Comanche village of Chief Iron Jacket in May 1858. In the battle that followed, the Texans killed 76 Comanches, including Iron Jacket, who was shot by the Tonkawa chief Placido, and captured 18 at a cost of only 2 dead and 2 captured. Prisoners told Ford that Buffalo Hump had a village only twelve miles away, but the victors were too tired to risk another fight. They returned to Texas, not having brought an end to raiding but having demonstrated that raiders could no longer find haven outside the state.[240]

John S. (Rip) Ford. *Courtesy of the Texas Ranger Hall of Fame and Museum.*

The Committee of Public Safety authorized the recruiting of volunteer troops during late February and March 1861. Colonels Henry McCulloch, younger brother of Ben, and John S. (Rip) Ford each recruited a regiment of cavalry. McCulloch, serving in central Texas, signed up ten companies of mounted troops known as the First Texas Mounted Rifles, the first military unit from Texas to enter Confederate service.[241]

The colorful Rip Ford, already a legend for his exploits as a ranger, soldier and explorer, recruited five hundred volunteers in the Houston area. Under Ford's leadership, these troops sailed to the mouth of the Rio Grande, where in late March they captured the Union outpost at Fort Brown. Ford was made commander of the lower Rio Grande district with headquarters in Brownsville. During 1861 and 1862, he constructed coastal defenses, negotiated trade agreements with Mexican authorities and fought his old nemesis, Mexican outlaw Juan (Cheno) Cortina.[242]

CHARLES DEMONTEL

Charles S. DeMontel met Henri Castro and joined his employ as an aide, guide and land surveyor in 1839. He led colonists from Indianola to the Castro land grant in 1844. At the conclusion of the Mexican War, in 1848, DeMontel commanded a company of Texas Rangers camped on Seco Creek near D'Hanis. In 1849, the site became Fort Lincoln. In 1853, he acquired fifteen thousand acres of land in the Hill Country in partnership with John Hunter Herndon and John James. Together, James and DeMontel surveyed and platted a town site; constructed a commissary, sawmill and cabins; and helped to sponsor many of the Polish settlers in what soon became the town of Bandera.[243]

He was appointed by Brigadier General Hamilton P. Bee to the position of provost marshal of Bandera, Uvalde and Medina Counties. By appointment of Governor Francis R. Lubbock, he also served as captain of Company G (later changed to D), Mounted Rangers, for Bandera, Blanco, Medina and Uvalde Counties in the Frontier Regiment. In this role, DeMontel was in command of the Texas Ranger post at Camp Verde. He was discharged from service on February 9, 1863, and commissioned by Jefferson Davis on March 14, 1863, as commander of the steamer *Texas*, a privately owned vessel of the Confederate States. In 1864, DeMontel returned to Medina County and raised a company of cavalry to serve under Colonel John S. (Rip) Ford. William (Big Foot) Wallace was his lieutenant.[244]

9

The U.S. Army in Texas

At the close of the Mexican War in 1848, troops of the United States were withdrawn from Mexico and assembled in Texas. Under the provisions of the Treaty of Guadalupe Hidalgo, the United States was duty bound to keep Indian raiders out of Mexico. The War Department reorganized the army and its military geography to protect the newly acquired western frontier. This new land was a vast territory increasing the domain of the United States by one-third. The Department of Texas, under the command of Colonel and Brevet Major General William Jenkins Worth, was assigned 14 percent of the regular army. Twenty-two companies of the U.S. Army were assigned to prevent raids against the Mexican nation and Texan settlers.[245]

In February 1849, General Worth issued General Orders No. 13, the original mission statement for Texas troops. He ordered his unit commanders to protect the lives and property of citizens, to prevent "as far as practicable" Indians from the United States crossing to raid into Mexico and, finally, to protect non-hostile Indians against violence and injustice. The mission General Worth set into motion was to remain the basic operational orders of army troops in Texas for the entire period of the Indian Wars.[246]

MISTAKES WERE MADE

Between 1848 and 1851, infantry troops established a string of company-sized posts along the frontier line. This became known as the First Federal Line. In 1851, Colonel Persifor F. Smith took command of Texas and immediately designed a new system of forts, eventually called the Second Federal Line. This new outer line of infantry-manned forts was one hundred miles in advance of the settlement line—roughly the edge of the Staked Plains and the Edwards Plateau. The fatal flaw in this strategy was the fact that the plan left the initiative entirely up to the Indians, who would strike at a time and place of their own choosing. It was not until after the Civil War that a new strategy of "large-scale converging-column" expeditions became the solution to the success of the Indian Wars in Texas.[247]

FIRST FEDERAL LINE, 1845–1849

1845: San Antonio–Camp Béxar. Established by the Second Dragoons on October 20, 1845, it served as Texas departmental headquarters because of its central strategic location and remained the preeminent military site in nineteenth-century Texas. It eventually became Fort Sam Houston–The Alamo. The Spanish mission San Antonio de Valero was leased by the departmental quartermaster and used for storage.

1848: Fredericksburg–Fort Martin Scott. Originally named Camp Houston, this post was established by the First U.S. Infantry on December 5, 1848.

1849: Burnet–Fort Croghan. Established three miles south of Burnet on March 18, 1849 by the Second Dragoons.

1849: D'Hannis–Fort Lincoln. Lieutenant James Longstreet and the Eighth Infantry established this as a post—Camp Seco—on July 7, 1849. Located on Seco Creek, two miles south of D'Hannis, this post was abandoned on July 20, 1852.

1849: Eagle Pass–Fort Duncan. This post on the Rio Grande near Paseo del Aquila or Eagle Pass was established by the First U.S. Infantry on March 27, 1849.

1849: Uvalde–Fort Inge. Established by the First U.S. Infantry on March 13, 1849, on the Leona River, one mile south of present Uvalde, the army abandoned this post on March 19, 1869.

After 1849, the line of forts along the 100th meridian could not and did not protect either Texas or the Mexican frontier. The military was under orders not to fight Indians unless it found them actually raiding. The Comanches did not fight the army posts, and troops were not attacked in Texas as the garrison line was fixed. The Comanche bands bypassed these army posts to burn, kill and plunder both Tejanos and the Mexicans.[248]

Second Federal Line, 1850–1859

1851: Mason–Fort Mason. Established on July 6, 1851, by the Second Dragoons, it served as headquarters for the Second U.S. Cavalry Regiment. It was abandoned on March 23, 1869.

1852: Bracketville–Fort Clark. Established on Las Moras Creek on June 20, 1852, by the First U.S. Infantry.

1852: Junction–Fort Terrett. Located twenty-five miles from present-day Junction on the North Fork of the Llano River, it was established by the First U.S. Infantry on February 5, 1852. The post was abandoned on February 26, 1854.

1852: Menard County–Fort McKavett. Established as a regimental camp on March 14, 1852, by the Eighth U.S. Infantry, this post was closed on June 30, 1883.

1855: Kerr County–Camp Verde. Established by the Second Cavalry on July 8, 1855, on the northern bank of Verde Creek just outside Bandera Pass, at the junction of the Comanche Trace and the old Spanish trail to Mission San Sabá.

1855: Bandera Pass–Camp Davant. Established in 1855 by one company of Mounted Rifles, under the command of Lieutenant J.H. Edson.

1857: Real County–Camp Wood. Established by the First U.S. Infantry on May 20, 1857, on the headwaters of the Nueces River near the present-day town of Camp Wood, John Bell Hood of the Second Cavalry commanded here in 1860.

1859: Kerr County–Camp Ives. A sub-post of Camp Verde established on October 2, 1859, by the Second Cavalry, it was located six miles south of Kerrville on the Lower Turtle Creek near the present-day crossing of SH 173.

U.S. SECOND DRAGOONS

After the annexation of Texas to the United States in the 1840s, the federal government became responsible for the protection of the frontier settlers from deadly raids by Indians and brigands. At the end of the Mexican War in 1848, the U.S. Army's Second Dragoons stayed in Texas from 1848 to 1855.[249] These troops were essential to the development of the Texas frontier, and what is now Kerr County was right on the edge of that frontier.

On January 12, 1853, Lieutenant Colonel St. George Cooke, commander of the Second Dragoon Regiment, engaged the Lipan Apaches near the headwaters of the Guadalupe River.[250] The site of this battleground is near the Kerr Wildlife Management Area on FM 1340, some twenty miles west of Kerrville (30°3.658'N, 99°30.249'W).

Trained to fight mounted or on foot, dragoons were superb in unconventional warfare. Unlike John Wayne's Cavalry that charged with pennants flying and bugles sounding, the dragoons went in very heavily armed and were skilled at stealthy infiltration—the "Special Forces" of the Hill Country. There were no Napoleonic battlefield formations here. These troopers would make slashing attacks with massive firepower, overwhelming the enemy with shock and awe. Their esprit de corps resulted from their exploits on the battlefield. The dragoons took great pride in their orange piping and hat cords, which set them apart from the cavalry.[251]

Troopers of the Second Dragoons in Texas were stationed at the following frontier posts in January 1850: Company A was at Fort Croghan in Burnet, Company B at Fort Martin Scott in Fredericksburg and Company C at Fort Inge in Uvalde. Also located in Texas were Company F at Fort Worth, Company G at Fort Lincoln in D'Hannis and Company I at Fort Graham in Hillsboro.[252]

As the frontier was pushed relentlessly westward, some army posts were bypassed and abandoned. During the year 1853, Forts Croghan, Graham, Worth and Martin Scott were forsaken in Texas. The mission of the dragoons shifted, and protection of the westward-bound wagon trails became imperative. At the end of that year, the companies in the Hill Country were stationed as follows: Company A at Fort Mason, F at Fort McKavett and G at Fort Terrett—all along the trail west.[253]

Fort Mason—at the village of Mason—was the center of dragoon operations in the Hill Country. Fort Mason's location on Post Oak Hill (30°44.362'N, 99°13.795'W), near Comanche and Centennial Creeks in the northern part of what was then Gillespie County, was chosen by

Second U.S. Dragoons, 1848. *Watercolor by Henry Alexander Ogden, published by U.S. Quartermaster General, 1890.*

Lieutenant Colonel William J. Hardee on July 6, 1851. Hardee left the actual establishment of the post to Brevet Major Hamilton W. Merrill and Companies A and B of the Second Dragoons. With the withdrawal of the Second U.S. Dragoons, Fort Mason became the headquarters for the U.S. Army Second Cavalry in 1856.[254]

The United States Army built Fort McKavett as part of its effort to protect the immigrant settlements and travelers on the "upper road" from San Antonio to El Paso in the 1850s. The Second U.S. Dragoons built many of the officers' quarters and barracks of the pre–Civil War Fort McKavett overlooking the headwaters of the San Saba River. Fort McKavett State Historic Site is a state park located twenty-three miles west of Menard (30°49.621′N, 100°6.578′W).[255]

Fort Terrett is located on the banks of the North Llano River in eastern Sutton County (30°27.623′N, 100°11.205′W). It was established on February 2, 1852, by Lieutenant Colonel Henry Bainbridge. This fort was also known as "Fort Lugubre" and the "Post on the North Fork of Llano River." The camp was established to protect the settlements along the San Antonio Road from Comanches. It was abandoned by federal troops on February 26, 1854. The State of Texas erected a marker in 1936 at the site, twenty-six miles from Junction off U.S. Highway 290W. Today, the old fort buildings are headquarters of the Nolan Ryan Ranch.

Dragoons would regularly patrol from these army posts, covering vast distances. It was not unusual for a mounted patrol to cover three hundred miles or more. The army infantry would garrison the forts. The First U.S. Infantry was one of the original units constructing and operating these outposts. These dragoons and infantry had fought side by side in the Mexican War.

The Second Dragoons carried the distinctive shortened rifle, called a musketoon. The U.S. Model 1847 cavalry musketoon was manufactured from 1848 to 1854 at the U.S. Springfield Arsenal. This was the first official percussion musketoon produced by the United States that was not a flintlock or conversion. It was a .69-caliber percussion (cap and ball) muzzleloader. Officers would often instruct their men to load these musketoons with a double charge: two .63-caliber balls and six .31-caliber buckshot (known as buck and ball).[256]

The Second Dragoons also were equipped with the Colt Dragoon handgun, carried in a saddle holster. It was a percussion revolver also known as a "cap n' ball" revolver. Its ammunition was in three components: the percussion cap, the ball shot and the black powder. It was a six-shot revolver and was one of the most powerful handguns of its day. The Colt Dragoon saw a lot of active service during war with Mexico. The huge Colt, with its tremendous stopping power, continued to be carried by the Texas Rangers fighting the Apaches and Comanches. The firepower of the Colt Dragoon .44 percussion revolver in the 1850s is on par with today's modern .357 Magnum.

Dragoons also carried the Ames Model 1840 cavalry saber (Old Wrist Breaker). Designed for slashing, the M1840 had a ridge around its quillon, a leather grip wrapped in wire (rather than grooves cut into the wooden handle) and a flat, slotted throat. It was forty-four inches long with a thirty-five-inch blade and weighed roughly two and a half pounds.

The Second Dragoons were withdrawn from Texas in 1855. This regiment had a record of distinction in the Texas Indian Wars. They went on to fight in the Indian Wars on the Great Plains. Today, the Second Dragoons continue to serve the U.S. Army as the Second Stryker Cavalry Regiment in Afghanistan.

U.S. Eighth Infantry Regiment

On the eve of the war against Mexico, the Eighth was transferred to Texas. The regiment fought with General Zachary Taylor's army as he drove south from Corpus Christi to Monterrey, taking heavy losses but winning high regard for its role in eight engagements against Mexican troops. After the war, the Eighth Infantry was deployed in Texas and New Mexico against various groups of Apache Indians. Organized into ten companies, the regiment was assigned the primary responsibility for protecting the trail between San Antonio and Santa Fe. By January 1849, the Eighth was distributed among the forts and camps of Texas, occupying them for the next twelve years. Among the posts of the Eighth Infantry was Camp Verde.[257]

Lieutenant James Longstreet came to Texas in 1849 and was assigned to Company G of the Eighth Infantry. He spent the summer of 1849 at Fort Lincoln, southeast of Camp Verde. Longstreet was later assigned to Fort Martin Scott at Fredericksburg in 1851.[258]

JOSÉ POLICARPO RODRÍGUEZ

José Policarpo (Poli) Rodríguez, scout and minister, was born at Zaragoza, Coahuila, Mexico (thirty-five miles west of the site of present-day Eagle Pass, Texas), on January 26, 1829. The Rodríguez family was of means and well educated. In 1841, the family moved to San Antonio, Texas, where the elder Rodríguez worked as a gunsmith for three years. Poli was employed as a surveyor for some years and worked in the Hill Country of Texas.[259]

In 1849, the twenty-year-old Poli was hired as a scout for the Whiting and Smith expedition, a government-contracted venture charged with establishing a westward road from San Antonio to El Paso. The expedition departed Fredericksburg on February 21 of that year, reached Presidio del Norte on March 25, proceeded north along the Rio Grande and finally reached El Paso on April 11. Since the last leg of the journey was marked by exceedingly difficult traveling conditions and Indian attacks, the Whiting party chose a more direct route back to San Antonio and arrived there on May 25. This latter route, laid out with the invaluable help of Poli Rodríguez, became the principal westward road to El Paso. The expedition also established Rodríguez's reputation as a reliable scout, and he continued to serve the government in this capacity until 1861.[260]

In the fall of 1854, Rodríguez had the distinction of being the guide for Brevet Major General Persifor F. Smith when he traveled through western Texas looking for a site for a new military post. The site Smith selected was called Fort Davis. Four years later, Rodríguez led a successful detail to find a number of camels that had escaped from their keepers at Camp Verde, Texas. The army was testing camels to see if they could be used to haul supplies on the western deserts. Rodríguez not only recovered all the camels but also came back to the post laden with bear, deer and turkey killed along the way.[261]

In 1856, Poli was transferred to Camp Verde in Kerr County, and two years later, he purchased 360 acres of land in Bandera County on Privilege Creek. There he built his home and ranch (29°46.46′N, 98°59.43′W). During the Civil War, Rodríguez refused a commission in the CSA and served as a private in the Bandera Home Guards. He was converted from Catholicism to Methodism and was granted a license to preach in 1878. In 1882, Rodríguez built on his land a small chapel, known as Polly's Chapel, where he acted as minister. He also donated land and oversaw construction of a one-room schoolhouse. Late in life, he published his autobiography, *The Old Guide* (1897).[262] Rodríguez died on March 22, 1914, in Poteet, Texas. In 1989, a fictionalized account of his life was published as the novel *Poli*, by Jay Neugeboren.[263] A descendant, Rudi R. Rodriquez, edited Poli's biography in a publication entitled *A Tejano Son of Texas: An Autobiography by José Policarpo "Polly" Rodriguez*.[264]

10

Camp Davant

Concerned about Indian depredations in the Camp Verde area, Governor Pease wrote to General T.F. Smith stating that there were no United States troops stationed in the vicinity and no actions had been taken against the Indians in the last eighteen months. Governor Pease went on to speculate that another raid by the Indians "would enrage the citizens so that they may arm themselves and do such violence to the Indians that a general war would result." He requested that General Smith station troops on the Upper Guadalupe.[265]

A little-known military outpost in Bandera Pass was established in 1855 by one company of Mounted Rifles under command of Lieutenant J.H. Edson.[266] It was later named Camp Davant in honor of Lieutenant William M. Davant, class of 1852, an officer in the Texas Mounted Volunteers who was killed during the Callahan Expedition on October 1, 1855. His unit was ambushed by Lipan Apache Indians while crossing the Rio Grande near Fort Duncan.[267]

Captain James Hughes Callahan

Governor E.M. Pease commissioned Captain James Hughes Callahan to form a company of rangers to pursue Indians, "follow them up, and chastise them wherever they may be found." Callahan's new company mustered at

Camp Davant in Bandera Pass on July 20, 1855 (29°51.221'N, 99°6.21'W). This was most likely the site of a Texas Ranger Cemetery, now called Bandera Pass Cemetery.[268]

In September 1855, the Callahan Expedition prepared for an invasion of Mexico. Under the command of Captain Callahan, a force of three companies of Texas Rangers, some 111 men, prepared to march into Nuevo León y Coahuila to punish Lipan Apaches. These Apaches had increased their raids that summer of 1855 when 3,000 United States troops were moved from the Texas frontier to Kansas. The Lipans had been raiding in this part of Texas all summer and into the fall of 1855 and then retreating across the border into Mexico near Piedras Negras.[269]

During that summer, many newspapers in the region were advocating for a military "filibustering" expedition into north Mexico, which was experiencing insurrectionist violence. At this time in history, a filibuster was someone who engages in an unauthorized military expedition into a foreign country to foment or support a revolution. To the public, this appeal became intertwined with Callahan's stated mission of chastising the Lipan Apaches.[270]

Captain William R. Henry

This perception was reinforced when troops, led by Captain William R. Henry, joined forces with the Callahan Expedition. Henry was a notorious filibusterer, adventurer and Texas Ranger. In July 1855, he organized a company of volunteers to intervene in Mexico and establish a government that would not threaten Texas interests. In letters to General Santiago Vidaurri, the governor of Nuevo León and one of the most powerful men of northern Mexico, Henry volunteered his services to support Vidaurri. The general was in a state of quasi revolution against the Supreme Government of Mexico and was in control of Nuevo León. Henry and others presumed that Vidaurri wanted to secede from Mexico and establish a republic of the Sierra Madre. Although Vidaurri declined the offer, Henry's forces pushed on, joining up with the Callahan Expedition at Leona, in present-day Uvalde County.[271]

FUGITIVE SLAVES

More significantly, the Callahan Expedition is said to have been an attempt by Texas slaveholders to regain fugitive slaves who had fled to northern Mexico and to prevent Mexican authorities from permitting runaway slaves to settle in their midst. Texas slave owners, meanwhile, had developed plans to capture fugitive slaves who had taken up refuge in northern Mexico, especially near San Fernando, Coahuila.[272] John S. (Rip) Ford estimated that more than four thousand slaves had run away from Texas by 1855. Ford was one of two agents appointed to negotiate with General Vidaurri.[273]

In the summer of 1855, the slave owners sent emissaries to talk with Vidaurri, but the governor rebuffed the offer and warned his military commanders on the frontier to be ready for an invasion. The slave owners apparently contacted Callahan and persuaded him to use his force to chastise the Mexicans, as well as Indians, and perhaps to capture fugitive slaves. Callahan's mission kept creeping ever larger.

CALLAHAN EXPEDITION INVADES MEXICO

Three companies of Texas Rangers departed Bandera Pass and passed through Uvalde. There, Captain Henry's filibustering forces joined up with Callahan. Captain Nathaniel Benton also arrived with another company of volunteers from Seguin. They had intended to enter Mexico at Los Moras Creek, but due to high water, the Texans crossed at Piedras Negras, Mexico—opposite modern-day Eagle Pass. The combined forces reached the international border on September 29. Callahan crossed the swollen Rio Grande on October 1–3. The filibusters made a separate crossing.

Captain Callahan was determined to press on directly to the Lipan Apache camp, near San Fernando, Coahuila, the home of a large number of runaway slaves from Texas. With 111 rangers and volunteers, Callahan advanced westward on October 3. The Texans collided with a Mexican detachment of 1,200 troops and Indians at the Río Escondido, about twenty-two miles from Piedras Negras. The enemy troops formed up in Callahan's front, throwing both wings forward and refusing their center. Instead of a flanking movement, Callahan attacked the Mexican center in a furious charge. In the ensuing battle, Callahan broke the Mexican line, seizing three Mexican cannons and ammunition. He then disengaged, pulled back to the Rio Grande River and took position at Piedras Negras, "prepared to fight against any odds that might come." He expected the worst, as the countryside was in pandemonium.[274]

In his letter to the people of Texas—written on October 4, 1855—Callahan pleads, "Men of the frontier, come then and help us. Let none come but those who will and can fight. If you come, come quickly; and come well prepared." This letter, with a detailed account of the expedition, was published in full in the *New York Times* on October 26, 1855.[275]

Burning of Piedras Negras

As the Mexican forces approached the town on October 5, Callahan ordered his men to set fire to buildings to cover their retreat. The town of Piedras Negras, Coahuila, was torched as the Callahan Expedition prepared to withdraw across the Rio Grande River.

On the evening of October 6, Major Sidney Burbank, commander of the American forces across the river at Fort Duncan, turned four cannons to cover the ground between the two opposing forces. While it has been said that the U.S. forces provided covering fire, in reality, Major Burbank told Callahan that if he tried to attack the Mexican forces, the U.S. artillery would fire on Callahan's troops. The presence and field of fire of the artillery convinced the opposing forces to cease and desist. Major Burbank did not fire but did furnish boats for Callahan's retreat across the Rio Grande.

Callahan immediately defended his invasion of Mexico, claiming that he had received permission from the Mexican authorities to cross the river in pursuit of the Lipans. Governor Pease defended Callahan's burning of Piedras Negras, saying that it was justified because the Mexicans had deceived Callahan by leading him into an ambush. Callahan's command was mustered out and disbanded.

A resident of Blanco County, Captain Callahan was killed there in April 1856 during a feud with Woodson Blassingame. The legislature of 1857–58 named Callahan County in his honor. He is now buried in the Texas State Cemetery.

11

The Second United States Cavalry

The story of the Second Cavalry Regiment of the United States Army presents the most enduring frontier history of the Verde Valley. This legendary regiment will forever be linked to the old army post at Camp Verde.

Jeff Davis's Own

Indian raids had become increasingly severe in the early 1850s. Settlers were confronted by the terrifying peril of horrific Indian attacks from Comanche, Lipan Apache and Kiowa raiding parties. In response to this frontier warfare, the Second United States Cavalry was organized specifically for service on the Texas frontier. Jefferson Davis, secretary of war for President Franklin Pierce, personally handpicked the officers of the Second Cavalry.[276]

Known as "Jeff Davis's Own," most of the officers, like Davis, were West Point graduates and southerners. The regiment was renowned for the sixteen general officers produced in the six and a half years of its existence. Eleven of these became Confederate generals, and the Second Cavalry supplied one-half, or four, of the full generals of the Confederate army: Albert Sidney Johnston, Robert E. Lee, Edmund Kirby Smith and John Bell Hood. Earl Van Dorn became a major general in the Confederate forces. George H. Thomas stayed with the U.S. Army, becoming a major general and commander of the Army of the Cumberland.[277]

Cavalry trooper. *By Frederic Remington.*

Equipment for the newly formed Second Cavalry was the subject of a Cavalry Equipment Board study. Three squadrons of the regiment were armed with the Springfield rifled carbine. One squadron of the Second Cavalry was armed with movable-stock carbine with the barrel ten or twelve inches long. Another squadron of the Second Cavalry was armed with the breech-loading Perry carbine. Colt .36-caliber navy revolvers and dragoon sabers were issued to all troopers.[278] Horses were purchased in Ohio, Indiana and Kentucky at an average price of $150. Camp Verde's Company D rode bays, as did Company I. Other companies of the Second Cavalry had horses of different coloring.[279]

To add further distinction, the War Department specified that the uniform jacket have yellow trim instead of the orange of the dragoons or the dark green of the Mounted Rifles. The stripes on the uniform trousers were also yellow. This uniform specification began the "yellow leg" tradition of the cavalry.[280]

The Second Cavalry Regiment, numbering 750 men and eight hundred horses, departed Fort Jefferson, Missouri, on October 27, 1855. The route passed through Missouri, Arkansas and Oklahoma and into Texas, arriving at Fort Belknap on December 27. Enduring freezing weather consistent with the "Little Ice Age,"[281] with temperatures well below zero, the Second Cavalry had 113 oxen freeze to death the night they arrived at Fort Belknap.[282]

Upon encampment of the Second Cavalry at Fort Belknap, orders were received assigning the companies to stations. The regimental headquarters, with Companies B, C, D, G, H and I, were directed to occupy the old post of Fort Mason on the Llano River (present-day Mason). Companies A, E, F and K were directed to establish a station, named Camp Cooper, near the Comanche Reservation on the Clear Fork of the Brazos.

The Second Cavalry spent five and a half years in Texas, serving out along the hazardous frontier. Davis named Colonel Albert Sidney Johnston the first commander of the Second Cavalry, which was commanded at various times by George H. Thomas, Earl Van Dorn and Robert E. Lee. The Second was Lee's last command in the United States Army.[283]

Lieutenant Colonel Robert E. Lee

Robert E. Lee arrived in Texas as part of the Second Cavalry Regiment as the second highest-ranking officer after Colonel Johnston. He soon assumed command of the regiment in San Antonio in May 1857.

Lieutenant Colonel Lee quickly grasped the theater of operations. Plans for extensive patrolling, rapid communications, frequent contacts and reliefs and strong reserves for possible pursuits were carefully prepared. The new strategy was to cover the entire frontier by continuous scouting of each river crossing, bank and bottom. The patrols were scheduled so that they appeared random and without pattern. More importantly, for the first

Lieutenant Colonel Robert E. Lee. *Courtesy of Texas Beyond History.*

time, these patrols were ordered to be aggressive. Whenever the troopers cut a trail, they were to immediately pursue and destroy the Indians in battle—search and destroy. The typical Second Cavalry patrol traversed six hundred miles and remained in the field for thirty days.[284]

CAMP VERDE, U.S. ARMY

For the purpose of providing additional protection to the settlements of the frontier, the companies of the Second Cavalry were dispersed to various stations. Company D was to take station at the old Spanish site at Campo Verde, at the foot of Monte del Mesa (29°53.491′N, 99°7.241′W). The U.S. First Infantry had already undertaken work on this station in 1855. Realizing the inefficiency of such a force on the frontier, the First Infantry was recalled in 1856. Captain Innis N. Palmer deployed with Company D of the Second Cavalry Regiment to develop Camp Verde, a United States Army frontier post, on July 8, 1856, on the northern bank of Verde Creek, three miles outside Bandera Pass in southern Kerr County. Camp Verde, sometimes known as Fort Verde, became a permanent station.[285]

In the heart of the Hill Country, with abundant water and shade, mild summers and good grazing, Camp Verde was one of the most desirable posts in Texas, if not the entire trans-Mississippi area. Lined by ancient cypress trees, the crystal-clear waters of Verde Creek meandered their way past the army post before joining the Guadalupe River. Camp Verde was strategically located to guard Bandera Pass, as well as the village of Bandera to the south and Kerrville to the north.[286]

Post returns for Camp Verde[287] from July 1856 note the following:

> *Innis N. Palmer, Captain Second Cavalry, commanding Company D.*
> *William Chambliss, First Lt. Second Cavalry, Company D.*
> *Cornelius Van Camp, Second Lt., Second Cavalry, Company D, on detached service as scout.*

The August 1869 post returns for Camp [illegible] (Brevet Major) Henry C. Wayne had arriv[illegible] and civilian employees on August 24, 1856. [illegible]

The successive U.S. Army commanding [illegible] as follows:

July 1856 to May 1858: Captain I.N. Palmer, Second Cavalry
May to August 1858: Second Lieutenant W.M. Graham, First U.S. Artillery
August 1858 to February 1859: Captain J.H. King, First U.S. Infantry
February 21 to 29, 1859: Second Lieutenant J.H. Holman, First U.S. Infantry
March to June 1859: Second Lieutenant W.M. Graham, First U.S. Artillery
June 1859 to November 1860: Major S.P. Heintzelman, First Infantry

Innis N. Palmer. *From Wikipedia, the Free Encyclopedia.*

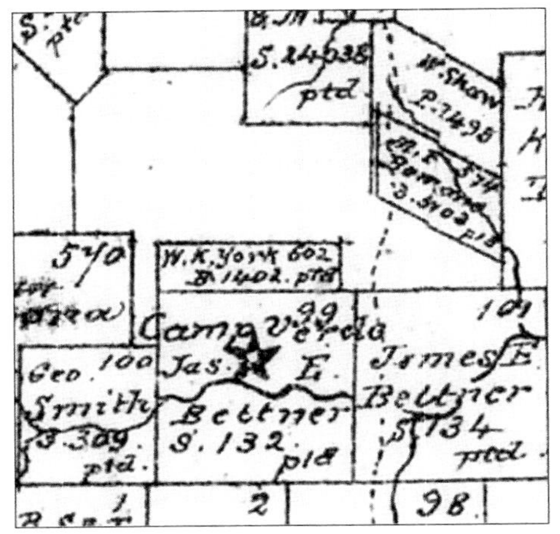

Left: Bettner Survey, 1854. *Bexar County Deed.*

Below: U.S. Army Map #15, Camp Verde. *The original is in the Records of the War Department, Headquarters of the Army Descriptive Book of the District of Texas, July 1, 1868, no. 220, National Archives of the United States.*

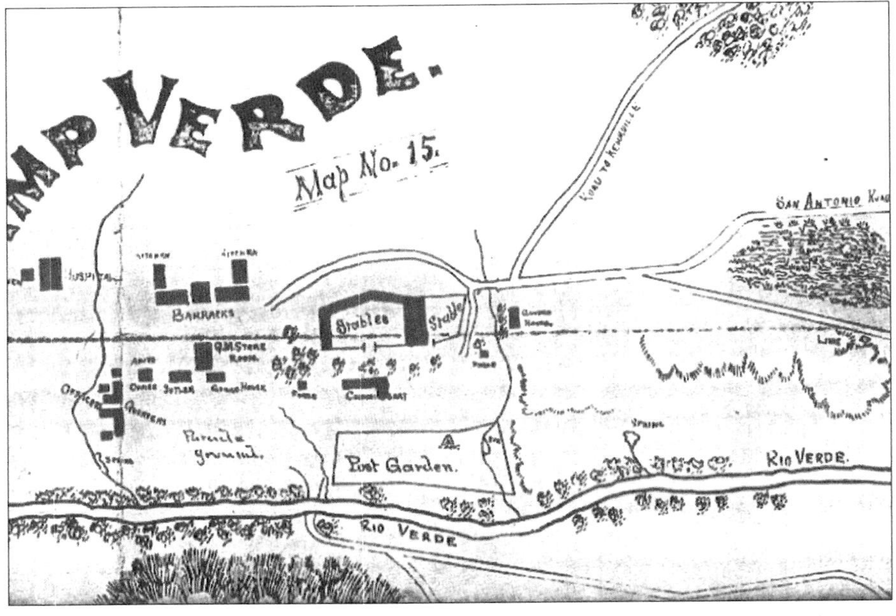

December 1860 to January 1861: Captain J.N. Caldwell, First Infantry
January to February 1861: Colonel C.A. Waite, First Infantry
February 18 to 28, 1861: Captain J.N. Caldwell, First Infantry

Camp Verde is on the National Register of Historic Places (73001968). It is presently on private land, inaccessible to the public. The National Register marker and a United Daughters of the Confederacy marker are on the remaining structure.

All that remains of the old garrison is the former officers' quarters building that is now used as a private residence. The building is visible from the turnout on the west Camp Verde Creek Road. This turnout also features the Texas State Historical Marker 4748, "Site of Camp Verde." In addition, there are two additional State Historical Markers: 680, "Camp Verde Barracks," and 682, "Camp Verde CSA," located in the historic park at the intersection of SH 173 and the east Verde Creek Road, in front of the Camp Verde Store. All of the latter are accessible to the public.

It is said that Robert E. Lee, being an army engineer, laid out the site plan for Camp Verde. This layout followed a standard design pattern that seldom varied significantly. An open rectangular parade ground formed the center of the post. Along one of the long sides of the rectangle stood officers' quarters. Enlisted barracks stretched the length of the other side. At some distance behind the barracks, troops constructed stables and a corral. Headquarters, hospital and quartermasters' buildings occupied the short sides of the parade ground. Kitchens, a powder magazine, a guardhouse, a post (sutler's) store and other assessor buildings stood away from the parade ground.[290]

Camp Verde. *Photo by Bryden Starr.*

E.C. Lane, better known as "Stuttering Lane," owned the sutler's store at Camp Verde.[291] The Williams community store was established a mile east of Camp Verde in 1857 in order to serve the needs of soldiers stationed there. It is reported that the primary purpose of John Williams's store was to provide liquor to the soldiers because regulations prohibited the sale of intoxicants within the camp. This store later became known as the Camp Verde Store, and a small community grew around the location. It is still in operation today.

It is important to observe that army posts, such as Camp Verde, were not intended to be fortresses with stockade walls. These forts and camps in Texas were intended to be bases for mobile operations. Camp Verde was a "minor fort." Patrols fanned out from Camp Verde, scouting trails, fords and water holes used by hostiles, including both Indians and outlaws.[292]

Second Cavalry officers and troopers patrolled in and around Kerr County, particularly along the old trail through Bandera Pass and beyond. Other trails that were scouted from Camp Verde included the Old Comanche Trace, the Old Spanish Trail to San Saba, trails upriver on the Guadalupe and the Frio Trail. The celebrated Robert E. Lee, then a lieutenant colonel in the United States Army, was at Kerrville, Center Point, Camp Verde and Camp Ives on numerous occasions.[293]

In 1856, there were reports of a large party of Indians near Camp Verde. Twenty-eight troopers and several civilians from the local area scouted unsuccessfully for the hostiles. The soldiers returned to Camp Verde while the civilians lingered in the area. The Indians attacked them while they slept in camp that night, killing four and wounding three. The wounded were taken to Kerrville, where one or two of the wounded later died. Upon hearing this news, Captain Palmer assembled a strong force of troops at Camp Verde and rode out in search of the warriors.[294]

First Sergeant Walter McDonald, with a detachment from Company D, departed Camp Verde in pursuit of Comanches on Kickapoo Creek. In combat on February 13, 1857, the Comanches were defeated with a loss of six warriors. One private was mortally wounded and died the next day at Fort McKavett. The bugler was severely wounded.[295]

Lieutenant Van Camp departed Camp Verde on October 29, 1857, with a detachment of Company D in pursuit of Comanches who had been attacking local settlements. He overtook the hostiles the next day on the Verde River. The chase covered six miles, over a terrain so rocky and rough that many of the troopers' horses were disabled, their shoes torn

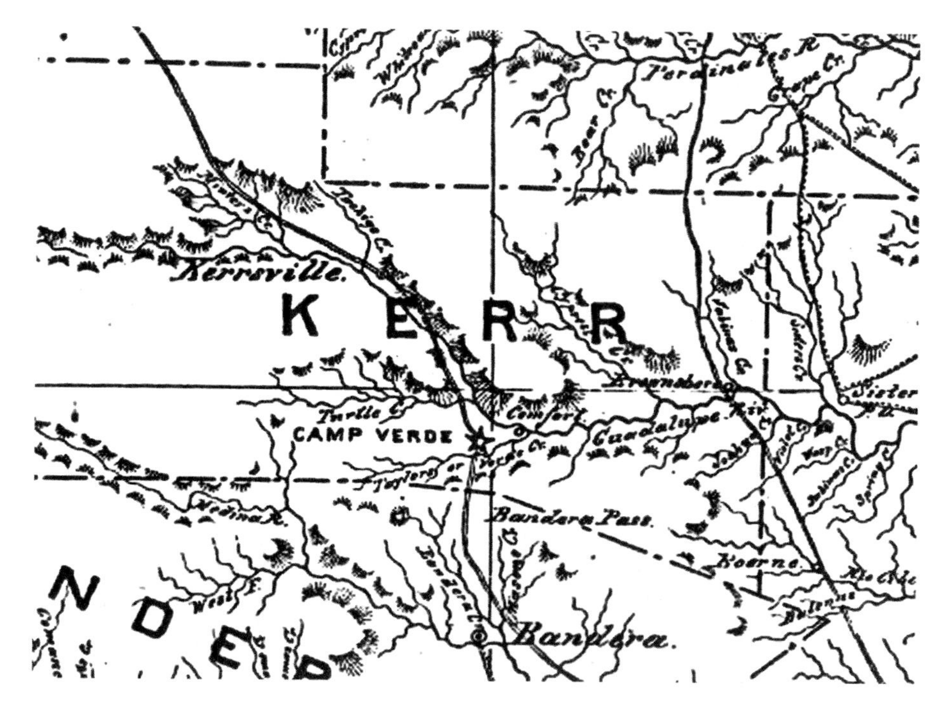

Map of Camp Verde and Environs. *1865 map of the state of Texas. Prepared under the direction of Brevet Major G.L. Gillespie, Captain Engrs. U.S.A., Chief Engineer, Military Division of the Gulf; compiled and drawn October 1865 and for stone June 1867 by Helmuth Holtz. Library of Congress, Geography and Map Division.*

from their hoofs. The soldiers wounded two Comanches and captured their property.[296] These troops were cited for valor. "The conduct of the troops is deserving of high praise for gallantry."[297]

The Comanches raided Kerrville in 1857, stealing horses and fleeing upriver. A posse of seven men pursued them to the vicinity of the Boneyard at the headwaters of the north fork of the Guadalupe River, the place the Spanish called Ojo de Agua de Guadalupe. Here the men camped and soon were attacked by the Comanches. In the ensuing fight, Dan Murff was killed, and the others made harrowing escapes downriver to Kerrville. A badly wounded Spencer Goss spent two weeks evading and escaping the Comanches. Newt Price died while trying to escape; his body was found two years later. Tom McAdams, Tom Wherry and William Kelso were also wounded but escaped. Shoeless, Jack Herridge limped back to Kerrville. By that time, the bottoms of his feet had come off.[298]

On January 25, 1858, First Sergeant Walter McDonald of Company D was dispatched from Camp Verde in pursuit of Comanche raiders who had been committing depredations on the San Jeronimo River. After a fast chase over four days, the troopers surprised the Comanches on the south branch of the Llano River. Two warriors were killed, and the stolen horses were recovered. Three privates were wounded.[299] Sergeant McDonald was cited for bravery: "This is the second time that the conduct of First Sergeant Walter McDonald, while on scouting duty, has elicited the mention of his name in orders. His energy and daring are eminently worthy of the emulation of every soldier in the department."[300]

Company D was stationed at Camp Verde until May 20, 1858, at which time it was relocated to Fort Belknap and ultimately to Camp Cooper. Troopers of the First U.S. Artillery and the First U.S. Infantry were stationed at Camp Verde.

The infantry troops were so ineffective that in the fall of 1859, the Second Cavalry created another post—Camp Ives—four miles north of Camp Verde. Company I was assigned to Camp Ives on October 2, 1859. Company I returned to Camp Verde on January 1, 1861, remaining there until the surrender of that post on February 21, 1861.[301]

Indians killed Roland Nichols of Kerrville in 1859. He is buried in the Nichols Cemetery between Kerrville and Ingram.[302]

In May 1859, Major Samuel P. Heintzelman had been given command of the First Infantry at Fort Duncan, near today's Eagle Pass. On June 25, Heintzelman received orders from General Twiggs to abandon Fort Duncan on the Rio Grande and transfer the First U.S. Infantry to Camp Verde. At the same time, Fort Brown at Brownsville, Ringgold Barracks at Rio Grande City and Fort McIntosh at Laredo were also ordered evacuated. These troops were needed farther west to combat the growing Indian problem on the frontier.[303]

Camp Verde appeared dilapidated, and Major Heintzelman set about rebuilding and repairing the facility. It was a pleasant experience at Camp Verde, with swimming in Verde Creek; hunting for deer, turkey and bear in the hills; and enjoying the produce of the camp's garden. The First Infantry band routinely provided concerts.[304]

Comanches continued to raid in the Camp Verde area, stealing horses and mules and taking captives. In response, Major Heintzelman sent out small detachments of the First Infantry in pursuit. It was no match in the rugged hills.

Heintzelman's journal provides a detailed and vivid account of the battles with Cortina's forces at El Ebonal and Rio Grande City, as well as glimpses into the filibustering activities of the Knights of the Golden Circle,[305] who were hoping to expand the Cortina War into a larger conflict that would lead to the eventual annexation of Mexico and the creation of a slave empire south of the Rio Grande. Heintzelman's impressions of his senior commander, Colonel Robert E. Lee, are also noteworthy.[306]

Camp Ives

Camp Ives was a military outpost four miles north of Camp Verde in southeastern Kerr County. Second Lieutenant Wesley Owens, commanding Company I, Second United States Cavalry, established the camp on October 2, 1859. Camp Ives, consisting of some twenty log cabins, was located on lower Turtle Creek (29°57.236′N, 99°6.24′W). The mission of Camp Ives was to protect the Military Road to Fort Terrett, as well as the Frio Trail.

On December 14, 1859, Corporal Patrick Collins, with a detachment from Company I, set out from Camp Ives in pursuit of Comanches. The troopers overtook the hostiles on the North Fork of the Guadalupe River. In the combat, four Comanches were killed, others were wounded and animals were captured.[307] The troopers were cited for valor: "Corporal Patrick Collins conducted the scout with discretion and energy, Privates Matthew Kennedy and Henry Weiss are specially mentioned. The men all behaved in the best manner." With these troopers was the celebrated guide from the Camp Verde area, José Policarpo (Poli) Rodríguez.[308]

The troopers of Camp Ives sortied with Lieutenant Colonel Robert E. Lee to the Rio Grande on March 13, 1860, returning on October 20, 1860, after a period of seven months.

In the face of imminent hostilities on January 28, 1861, this company was transferred to Camp Verde, and Camp Ives was abandoned. Camp Ives was used by the Confederates intermittently during the Civil War.[309]

Accomplishments of the Second Cavalry in Texas

During their stay in Texas, companies of the Second U.S. Cavalry Regiment were involved in some forty engagements along the western and northern frontiers of Texas and along the Rio Grande, fighting Apaches, Comanches, Kiowas and Mexican marauders. Various companies of the regiment also conducted numerous scouting expeditions into west and northwest Texas, some of five and six weeks' duration. The most significant engagement fought by the regiment in Texas was the Battle of Devil's River on July 20, 1857. On that date, Lieutenant John Bell Hood, with a detachment of twenty-five men from Company G, fought a combined force of Comanches and Lipan Apache warriors near the head of the Devil's River, south of Sonora.[310]

At the outbreak of the Civil War, the Second U.S. Cavalry Regiment was ordered out of Texas in late February 1861 and left the state via Indianola during March and April. When the mounted units of the United States Army were reorganized in the fall of 1861, the Second Cavalry became the Fifth Cavalry, the designation by which it is known today. The Second Cavalry had driven the Indians out of Kerr County; had fought the Comanches, Kiowas and Lipan Apaches deep in their heartland; and had made a significant contribution to Texas frontier history.

12

Camels

Camp Verde was the site of the famous U.S. Army Camel Experiment.[311] It is, perhaps, for this unique exploit that Camp Verde is most renowned. Senator Jefferson Davis, appointed secretary of war by President Franklin Pierce, had to cope with Indians and with transportation in Texas. At the perseverance of the War Department, Congress passed, on March 3, 1855, the Shield amendment to the appropriation bill, which made $30,000 available "under the direction of the War Department in the purchase of camels and the importation of dromedaries, to be employed for military purposes."

Major H.C. Wayne

On May 10, 1855, Major H.C. Wayne received a special presidential assignment. The naval store ship *Supply*, in command of Lieutenant D.D. Porter, was placed at Wayne's disposal. After a Middle Eastern shopping expedition, thirty-two camels, plus one calf born at sea, arrived at Indianola, Texas, on April 29, 1856. Wayne's camels passed through Bandera Pass on August 26 and 27, 1856, arriving at their new post at Camp Verde.[312] The animals were permanently stationed at Camp Verde (called Little Egypt), where several successful experiments were made to test the camels' utility in the pursuit of Indians and the transportation of burdens.[313]

Pack train of camels. Harper's Weekly, *June 30, 1877.*

With every camel outing, a teamster rode ahead, shouting, "Get out of the way, the camels are coming!" The camels frightened horses badly. One description noted that "the flat nostrils gave the beasts a disdainful look and the half-closed eyes and pouting lip lent a most bored and sleepy expression to the creatures."[314]

HI JOLLY

Little is known of the men who were hired to care for and drive these camels. In *Go West Greek George* by Steven Dean Pastis, these camel drovers were Hadji Ali (aka Hi Jolly, aka Philip Tedro), Yiorgos Caralambo (later known as Greek George), Mimico Teodora (Mico), Hadjiatis Yannaco (Long Tom), Anastasio Coralli (Short Tom), Michelo Georgios, Yanni IIlato and Giorgios Costi. Hadji Ali (Hi Jolly) was the lead camel wrangler during the U.S. Army's experiment in using camels in the dry deserts of the Southwest.[315]

By November 25, 1856, Hadji Ali was documented as a "camel herder" at Camp Verde, with a salary of fifteen dollars a month. He was hired to teach the Camp Verde soldiers how to pack and handle the animals. The troops had a hard time pronouncing Ali's name, so they nicknamed him "Hi Jolly."

Hi Jolly was born Philip Tedro, and he took the name Hadji Ali when he converted to Islam during his early life after making the pilgrimage to Mecca. He was born either somewhere in Syria or in Smyrna around 1828 and was of Greek and Syrian parentage. Hadji Ali was an Ottoman citizen. He worked for the Ottoman armed forces, and he was a breeder and trainer of camels. Hi Jolly later served with the French army in Algiers before signing on as a camel driver for the U.S. Army in 1856.

Lieutenant Edward Fitzgerald Beale, USA, used Ali's expertise at handling camels to haul supplies in Southern California and Arizona. After the U.S. Camel Experiment, Hadji Ali tried to run a freight business in Arizona using a few camels he kept. Unfortunately, the business failed, and Ali released his camels into the Arizona desert near Gila Bend.

In 1880, Hadji Ali became an American citizen and used the name Philip Tedro (sometimes spelled Teadrow). In his final years, Ali moved to Quartzsite, Arizona, where he mined and occasionally scouted for the U.S. government. He is reported to have been with the U.S. Army at Huachuca and other posts until the surrender of Geronimo and the last of the Chiricahua Apaches in 1886.

Philip Tedro died on December 16, 1902. According to local legends, repeated in the *Arizona Capital Times* in 1995, "The final, sad act of the drama occurred on Dec. 16, 1902 when 75-year-old Hi Jolly was sitting in a saloon at Quartzite, Ariz. A prospector stumbled in, telling of a huge, red camel wandering nearby. Hi Jolly rushed outside and was never seen alive again." One legend states that his withered body was found weeks later in the remote desert. There he lay, with lifeless arms wrapped around the neck of the last camel in the West. Another legend, published by Robert Froman in *American Heritage* in 1961, states that Hi Jolly, tied in the saddle, could be seen on a red camel, called the Red Ghost. The apparition appeared frequently during dust storms in the area. The tale of this ghost story has Hi Jolly riding the camel forevermore.[316]

The Arizona Highway Department has built a tomb for him—a pyramid of quartz and petrified wood topped by the figure of a camel. "The last camp of Hi Jolly," a sign reads. In death, the legend of Hi Jolly has quite literally saved a town and continues to give thousands of Americans an excuse to visit this historical marker. Ali's spirit lives on in the form of Hi Jolly Daze each year in Quartzite, Arizona. This "Camelmania" celebration features a parade, which starts at the post office and goes west to the rodeo grounds. Camel races follow.

Mimico Teodora (Mico) remained with the camels at Camp Verde. He built himself an adobe residence on the road to Bandera Pass, south of Verde Creek. When he died, his neighbors buried Mimico Teodora beside the creek that bears his name: Mico Creek.[317]

CONFEDERATE CAMELS

In early 1861, Texas seceded from the United States, and on February 28, the Texas Confederates seized Camp Verde. Eighty camels and two Egyptian drivers passed into Confederate hands. The surrender of Camp Verde to the Confederates is detailed in the book *With the Border Ruffians*, written by R.H. Williams, a Confederate sergeant who was present at the surrender:

> *A sergeants' guard received us and escorted us into the fort, outside which I saw strong picket defenses had been thrown up and I made sure we were in for a fight. Lieutenant Hill, the officer in command, received us very stiffly and said that he meant to hold his post to the last. He had received orders to retire, as we afterwards learned, but put on a better face to gain better terms...When* [Captain] *Paul offered to let all officers and men march out with their horses, arms and personal property, which was what he had been fighting for, Hill at once agreed and the terms were forthwith settled. Hill was to march out next day and report himself and his command at San Antonio. So at two o'clock that day, he marched out and we took possession of the fort, the stores, ammunition, twelve mules, eighty camels, and two Egyptian camel drivers, for all of which I had to give a receipt.*[318]

The camels soon were widely scattered. Some were set loose on the open range near Camp Verde, some were used to freight cotton bales from Kerr County to Brownsville and one camel found its way to the infantry command of Captain Sterling Price, who used it throughout the war to carry the whole company's baggage. Although the camels were put to limited use in Confederate Texas carrying salt, supplies and mail, no real plan for them was ever realized.

At the end of the Civil War, Major General David Sloane Stanley led the Fourth Corps into Texas in June 1865 to counter growing French involvement in Mexican internal affairs and the threat posed by the emperor Maximilian. While commandant at San Antonio, he ordered the sale of the remaining camels from Camp Verde.[319]

Many camels were sold to circuses in 1866. Some camels were eventually turned loose. It is said that the Indians gradually killed and ate some of the roving survivors, and others were shot at random, especially by cattlemen who had always hated the beasts for frightening their livestock. There is a Camp Verde landmark named Camels' Leap that, according to local folklore, was a precipice over which camels were driven to their death.[320]

So ended rather shabbily Jeff Davis's experiment of introducing the "ships of the desert" into our Southwest.[321]

13

The Surrender of Camp Verde, 1861

Kerr County was in conflict over secession in 1860, narrowly voting in favor of secession seventy-six to fifty-seven. Unionists from Kerr, Gillespie and Kendall Counties were among those who participated in the establishment of the Union League in the summer of 1861, and by the summer of 1862, they had formed militia companies to protect the frontier against Indians and their families against local Confederate forces.

General Twiggs

At department headquarters in San Antonio, General David Emanuel Twiggs, seventy-one and in ill health, was known to be sympathetic to the South but proud and protective of his command. On February 16, 1861, Colonel Benjamin McCulloch, a veteran of the Texas Revolution and the Mexican War who had been appointed a colonel of cavalry by a committee of the Secession Convention, swarmed into San Antonio's Main Plaza with 250 men and quickly occupied the rooftops of buildings housing Federal supplies and men. Carrying the Lone Star flag, McCulloch vowed that he would force General Twiggs to surrender. After ten days of tense negotiations, state commissioners persuaded Twiggs, who was said to have wept like a child, to turn over all Federal property in Texas. "If an old woman with a broomstick should come with full authority from the state of Texas to demand the public property," Twiggs was heard to say, "I would give it to her."[322]

San Antonio Plaza Square, looking away from the Alamo, celebrating the surrender of Twiggs. Harper's Weekly, *March 23, 1861.*

Under growing threats from militants in the Knights of the Golden Circle,[323] General Twiggs made numerous requests for instructions from the government, finally surrendering on February 18, 1861. He then issued an Order of Exercises, in which he required the U.S. troops to evacuate the posts and surrender all public property not necessary for transportation to Green Lake. There, the troops were to further surrender their transportation and wait for ships to evacuate them from Texas.[324] Green Lake is located at the mouth of the Guadalupe River (28°30.795′N, 96°51.22′W), less than three miles from the coast at San Antonio Bay and twelve miles west of Port Lavaca.[325]

Colonel Carlos A. Waite

On February 15, 1861, General Twiggs was relieved of his command. The command of the U.S. Army's Department of Texas devolved to Colonel Carlos Adolphus Waite, commanding the First Infantry at Camp Verde.[326] Colonel Waite had a low opinion of the defensibility of Camp Verde. The post was designed to function as a cavalry patrol base, not as a fortress.

Colonel Waite wrote to the U.S. Army Department of Texas at San Antonio on January 28, 1861:

> *The Camp* [Verde] *is spread over much ground, and is the most ill chosen and least defensible site I have ever seen selected for any military purposes. It is on ground that slopes down to Verde Creek, a stream that is fordable every few yards, and every part is exposed to high ground on the other side, which is within short rifle range, and which completely commands it.*

Twigg's surrender resulted in his dishonorable dismissal from the army.[327] Colonel Waite rode from Camp Verde by back roads into San Antonio only to find that chaos had engulfed the army command in San Antonio. Major Sacfield Maclin, who had gone over to the Texan Rebels, forced Colonel Waite to surrender after a heated and lengthy confrontation and debate. In the confusion, Corporal John C. Hesse was able to conceal and carry off the flag of the Eighth Infantry, which had been carried through the Mexican War. The flag, which Hesse had concealed around his body, was placed in Lieutenant Edward A. Hartz's trunk and taken to Washington. Hesse, who went on to become a colonel, later received the Medal of Honor for his patriotic deed.[328]

CAPTAIN JAMES PAUL

On the same day General Twiggs was relieved of command, Camp Ives was abandoned. Company I of the Second U.S. Cavalry reported to Camp Verde. On February 21, 1861, James Paul of the Castroville Castle of the Knights of the Golden Circle received a commission to raise a company of Texas Mounted Rangers. He enrolled twenty-six men and marched to Camp Verde. Paul's rangers arrived at Camp Verde on March 6, 1861, and negotiated the surrender of the garrison.[329] The next day, the Union troops departed in possession of all their arms, ammunition and horses. This small band of Texas Rangers then occupied Camp Verde, taking possession of twelve mules, eighty camels and two Egyptian drivers.[330]

Post Returns for April 1861

Under the command of Captain Palmer, the first contingent of the Second Cavalry, consisting of Companies D, B, H and I, sailed on the steamship *Coatzacoalcos* on March 31. Their evacuation route took these troops to Key West, Havana, New York and Carlisle Barracks in Pennsylvania. Company D was ordered to Washington, D.C., where it arrived on April 17.

The post return for Camp Verde, USA, for February 1861 reveals the following transitions:

James N. Caldwell, Capt. First Infantry, Post Commander, 26–28 February 1861.
Joseph A. Mower, First Lt., First Infantry, Post Commander, 23–25 February 1861.
Dr. Charles A. Ganahl, Post Physician.
Samuel P. Heintzelman Major, First Infantry, on leave since 17 December 1860.
Carlos A. Waite, Col., First Infantry, transferred to San Antonio.
Gouverneur Morris, Lt. Col., First Infantry, transferred to San Antonio.
Sidney Burbank, Major, First Infantry, transferred to San Antonio.
Albert G. Brackett, Capt., Second Cavalry, "took up the line of march for the coast on the 23rd inst. per Dept. General Order No. 5, dated San Antonio, Feby 18, 1861, Post Order No. 13 of Feby 13, 1861."
Charles W. Field, First Lt. Second Cavalry, transferred with his company.
T.W. Leftwich, First Lt. First Infantry, transferred to San Antonio.
Edwin D. Phillips, First Lt. First Infantry, transferred to San Antonio.
Wesley Owens, Second Lt. Second Cavalry, transferred with his company.

Assuming command on February 19 at San Antonio, Colonel Waite hoped that his widely scattered garrisons could rendezvous at Green Lake and carry out the terms of their transfer from the Lone Star State. News of the firing on Fort Sumter, however, convinced state officials to arrest Waite, along with most of his departmental staff, on April 23. Exchanged in early 1862, Waite found himself relegated to noncombat assignments. He retired from the army in 1864 and died two years later.[331]

On April 23, Texas called for the capture of all Federal military companies remaining in the state and for them to be given the choice of either joining the Confederacy or being imprisoned. Some of the remaining uncaptured companies elsewhere in the state attempted to flee to Green Lake, where they could safely wait to depart near an adequate source of fresh water. Soon after, a Confederate force entered the harbor and captured the remaining transport steamship, *Star of the West*, and all Union troops were taken as prisoners of war.[332]

LOOTING AT CAMP VERDE

On March 2, 1861, Colonel Waite, USA Commanding Department of Texas, was sent a letter from the Office of Commissioners in San Antonio. This letter complained, "After the departure of Capt. Macklin's company from Camp Verde, the soldiers of Company A. First Infantry, burned up a chest of saddler's tools belonging to the Federal Government, left by Capt. Brackett, to be placed in the quartermaster's store." The letter went on to note that "five days after, on the night of the return of that company to Camp Verde, the men broke into the hospital, and after consuming the liquor, destroyed all they could not conveniently appropriate to their own use; the night after, they broke into the carpenter's shop and destroyed everything that was not appropriated by them to their own use."[333]

Having received the reports of devastation at Camp Verde, the Texas Committee of Public Safety demanded that Colonel Waite remove, "without delay," the soldiers of Company A, First Infantry, United States Army. Company A from Camp Verde began its exodus from Texas in February 1861, marching to Green Lake. During their stay at Green Lake, Texas seceded from the Union. On March 30, they embarked to Key West, Florida. Captain Frank Hubert's company of Washington County volunteers, numbering twenty-five men under the command of Lieutenant Haynes, then in San Antonio, was directed to march the next morning for Camp Verde "and there remain for the protection of the public property and buildings until further notice."[334]

14

Camp Verde, CSA

Camp Verde became a Confederate army post. When the Union forces departed the garrison, it was deconstructed by local residents, who carted away almost anything movable. The looting must have been severe as the camp appeared in disarray, as reported by Captain Buquor. The Camp Verde army post was used intermittently by various Confederate forces during the Civil War. The Prison Canyon POW Camp operated with six hundred prisoners immediately across Verde Creek from Camp Verde. The Texas Rangers used another site some two miles downstream, at Nowlin's Ranch.

Among the Confederate forces operating in this area during the Civil War were Captain Stokely M. Holmes's Company of Wood's Regiment, the Thirty-sixth Texas Cavalry (often called the Thirty-second),[335] Captain John Donnelson's Company of the Second Texas Mounted Rifles, Captain James W. Duff's Company of Texas Partisan Rangers, Captain Henry D. Davis's Company of Texas State Troops, Captain Richard Taylor's Eighth Texas Cavalry Battalion and Colonel Philip N. Luckett's Third Texas Infantry.[336]

Among the irregular forces were Quantrill's Partisan Rangers and the infamous "hangerbande" (the hanging band or gang) that conducted terrorist raids throughout the area. James P. Waldrip, a farmer from northeast Gillespie County, met with some of William Quantrill's men, led by Bill Paul, who had come to Camp Davis fresh from atrocities in Kansas on a horse- and cattle-buying expedition. J.P. Waldrip organized

Quantrill's men and some of his friends to form the hangerbande. Camp Davis was one of the many camps that Duff's troops and Waldrip's hangerbande utilized, and hangings, in fact, were frequent.[337]

CAPTAIN PASQUALE LEO BUQUOR

When the Civil War broke out, former Texas Ranger Pasquale (Pasquier) Leo Buquor organized a volunteer company and served as captain. According to his war records, he mustered into Company A, Third Regiment Texas Infantry of the Confederate States Provisional Army, on May 25, 1861. He was ordered to Camp Verde to take command. His wife, Jesusa, and four children accompanied him to this post, arriving on June 1, 1861.[338]

Three days following Captain Buquor's arrival at Camp Verde, he wrote a report to Colonel Earl Van Dorn, Confederate Department of Texas, complaining about the "awful state of decay" of the post. He reported that Mr. McKee's men had turned the quarters into stables and, together with some neighbors, burned, stole and destroyed everything in the way of camp necessities. "The accumulation of filth about the premises was so incredible in so short a time." Captain Buquor went on to say, "A quantity of hospital stores were stolen from this Post by the hospital steward of the former Government named Hillard. Also, another individual named Ludovic Lang carried away a large amount of public property."[339]

Although Captain Buquor and his men did clean up the Camp Verde army post, a number of neighbors gave them considerable problems. Mr. Lang filed charges against Buquor for damages to his livestock. In response to these charges, Captain Buquor stated that upon arrival at Camp Verde, he had to employ one-half of his company in driving Lang's cattle and hogs from the post quarters. Buquor went on to report that at the time that Captain Caldwell abandoned the post, Lang "hauled away several wagon loads of Government property, such as the doors and windows of the soldiers' quarters, the barracks, mess tables benches, stores and a quantity of tools, blankets, hospital property, etc."[340]

Captain Buquor obtained search warrants in an effort to recover the property stolen by Ludovic and Hilliarn Lang. On June 22, Lang went to the post looking for Captain Buquor "in a menacing and threatening attitude armed with a double barrel shotgun, six shooter and Bowie knife, creating by his acts and language considerable uneasiness to my family." The next morning, Lang returned to the post and entered Captain Buquor's quarters demanding to know why Buquor had killed his cows. The captain seized Lang's gun, struck him over the head with it, disarmed him and had Mr. Lang escorted out of the camp, warning him to not return on threat of being "placed in irons." By the end of summer, the matter had been apparently dropped.[341]

Second Texas Mounted Rifles, CSA

The Second Texas Cavalry was also known as the Second Texas Mounted Rifles when the regiment was first organized in 1861. In 1862, the regiment was reorganized under the Second Texas Cavalry. These men lived in counties near San Antonio, Texas, when they enlisted.

The original field officers included Colonel John S. Ford, Lieutenant John R. Baylor, Major John Donelson, Major Matthew Nolan, Major Charles L. Pyron, Major William A. Spencer, Lieutenant Colonel James Walker and Major Edwin Waller Jr.

The Second Texas Cavalry participated in several engagements during the Civil War. The regiment fought at San Lucas Springs, Mesilla, San Augustine Springs, Fort Stanton, Fort Craig, Fort Bliss, Fort Thorn, Canada Alamosa, Camp Robledo and Fort Inge. In 1862, the unit was engaged in the Sibley campaign at the Battles of Valverde and Glorieta in New Mexico and Boutte Station and Bayou des Allemands in Louisiana. The Second Texas Cavalry returned to Texas, where it fought at Fort Clark near the Nueces River. The men were dismounted in March 1865 and gradually disbanded in mid-May as a substantial number fled across the Rio Grande into Mexico. The Second Texas Cavalry was officially surrendered with General Edmund Kirby Smith at Galveston on June 2, 1865.[342]

Texas Third Infantry Regiment, CSA

Colonel Phillip Nolan Luckett's Texas Third Infantry Regiment completed its organization during the fall of 1861 with recruits from Travis, Béxar,

Kerr and surrounding counties. Many German conscripts were from Gillespie County after the massacre of Germans fleeing to Mexico on the Nueces River by James Duff's irregular partisans. Luckett's regiment consisted of 648 effectives and was attached to Colonel John S. Ford's Western Subdistrict Companies from the Third Texas Infantry. This unit guarded the Camp Verde POWs early in the war. Later, the POW camp was garrisoned by elements of McCord's Frontier Regiment.[343]

THIRTY-SIXTH TEXAS CAVALRY

The Thirty-sixth Texas Cavalry was the highest officially numbered Texas cavalry regiment. The unit was organized on March 22, 1862, at Belton, Texas, and is often incorrectly confused with the Thirty-second and Fifteenth Texas Cavalries. The original officers included Colonel Peter C. Woods, Lieutenant Colonel Nathaniel Benton, Lieutenant William O. Hutchinson and Major Stokely M. Holmes. The Thirty-sixth Texas Cavalry consisted of ten companies that included 823 men from Bee, Bell, Béxar, Caldwell, Comal, DeWitt, Gonzales, Guadalupe, Hays and Hopkins Counties. The unit was known by several alternate names, including Woods's Cavalry, Benton's Cavalry, Holmes's Cavalry, Hutchinson's Cavalry and White's Cavalry. In the summer of 1862, the Thirty-sixth Texas Cavalry was stationed at Camps Bee, Clark, Frio, Hood, Magruder, Salado and Verde in Texas. It patrolled the Texas coast from Fredericksburg to Brownsville until July 1862. The soldiers protected cotton wagons going into Mexico to sell to English traders at Matamoros.[344]

CAPTAIN DUFF AND MARTIAL LAW IN KERR COUNTY

On April 28, 1862, Confederate general Hamilton Bee declared martial law, posting to Gillespie and Kerr Counties a detachment of partisan rangers. Captain James Duff was in command, given authority to do whatever was necessary to end the resistance of Unionists.

The martial law order required all males over sixteen to register with provost marshals and take an oath of allegiance to the Confederacy. Captain Duff ordered all men in the Hill Country to report to him within six days and take the required oath. Duff declared himself provost and then stated in a letter, "The God damn Dutchmen are Unionists to a man…I will hang all I suspect of being anti-Confederates." Duff arrested several local citizens and hanged two German immigrants he considered to be troublemakers. These incidents caused many Unionists to decide to flee to Mexico.[345]

Hangings were, in fact, frequent. Letters from German residents of Fredericksburg attest that many of them would leave their homes at sundown and hide in the surrounding woods in fear of "night riders," who snatched young men from their beds, hanged their parents and burned their homes for avoiding conscription.[346]

Captain James W. Duff used torture. To obtain information, his soldiers sometimes resorted to bullwhips; other times, they would hang a person by the neck and then release their victim just before strangulation, repeating the process until either the interrogation had been successful or the suspect was dead—not unlike modern-day water boarding. Duff is credited with killing over fifty men in the Hill Country. Some two thousand local residents took to the hills to escape Duff's reign of terror.[347]

Captain Henry T. Davis established Camp Davis on White Oak Creek in 1862 (30°11.617'N, 99°7.211'W). This was a major Confederate camp throughout the Civil War.[348] Also operating out of Camp Davis were minutemen irregulars under the command of Major James M. Hunter, as well as Captain Duff's forces. Later, a squad from William Quantrill's Raiders, led by Bill Paul, arrived at Camp Davis, fresh from Kansas atrocities. James P. Waltrip, of Fredericksburg, emboldened by the Quantrill men, organized his friends and the Quantrill men into the infamous hangerbande that conducted terrorist raids throughout the area. The Black Flag of Quantrill's Partisan Rangers meant "no quarter" for prisoners and was the most feared Confederate battle flag to Union soldiers. These troops became the core of Duff's counterinsurgency forces.[349]

Guido Ransleben's 1954 book, *A Hundred Years of Comfort in Texas*, includes a letter written in 1908 by Howard Henderson to J.W. Sansom that reads, in part:

> *I know that J.W. Duff and his company of murderers killed many of my neighbors and friends. My uncle and cousins, Schram Henderson, my wife's father and brother, Turknette, were murdered; Duff and his gang butchered all my neighbors, Hiram Nelson, Frank Scott and his father, Parson Johnson and old man Scott. Rocks were tied to their feet*

and they were thrown into Spring Creek. Their crime was failure to come in and pledge loyalty to the Confederacy within three days.[350]

Among those hanged in this incident was Gus Tegener, brother of Fritz Tegener. Unknown "bandits" hanged the third Tegener brother, William, and threw his body over a fifty- to seventy-five-foot bluff into the Guadalupe River below.

In 1862, the Union Loyal League met on Bear Creek, above Comfort. Some five hundred members took part in the gathering. Fritz Tegener, Kerr County treasurer, was elected major. All persons wanting to make a run for Mexico to escape further conscription were told to gather at the head of Turtle Creek, west of Kerrville (29°59′N, 99°18′W). On August 1, 1862, sixty-eight men—sixty-three Germans, one Mexican and four Anglos—heeded the call.[351]

BATTLE OF THE NUECES

The consequence of Duff's order was the infamous Battle of the Nueces, conversely known as the Nueces Massacre. Lieutenant Colin D. McRae was at Camp Pedernales—today's Morris Ranch (30°12.473′N, 98°58.734′W)—when he received orders from Captain Duff to wipe out any armed encampments in the area. Duff was emphatic in his directive of no prisoners.[352] McRae's command included ninety-four men who were detached from Captain John Donelson's Company of the Second Texas Mounted Rifles, Captain Duff's Fourteenth Texas Cavalry Battalion, Captain Henry D. Davis's Company of Texas State Troops and Richard Taylor's Eighth Texas Cavalry Battalion.

The Texans intercepted the Germans on the west bank of the Nueces River (twenty miles from Fort Clark) on August 10, 1862, at what was to become known as the Battle of the Nueces. In the skirmish, Duff's Fourteenth Texas Cavalry Battalion attacked and killed the majority of the fleeing immigrants.

Unsuspecting, outnumbered and outgunned, approximately thirty of Tegener's men were killed in the fighting, and twenty were wounded, captured and executed on the spot with a bullet in the back of the head. Six more were killed trying to escape across the Rio Grande. Of the twenty or so escapees who managed to flee for Mexico, seven or eight were killed by yet another patrolling Confederate force in October as they tried to cross the Rio Grande, and nine more were captured at various locations and executed out of hand.[353]

In 1865, the remains were returned and buried in a mass grave in Comfort. The next year, on August 10, 1866, the first monument in Texas was erected at the grave site to remember this grim battle. The Treue der Union, or True to the Union, Monument was a simple obelisk, inscribed with the names of the men who were killed. Outside National Cemeteries, this remains the only monument to the Union erected in a state south of the Mason-Dixon line.

This monument, listed on the National Register of Historic Places, is also noteworthy for another unusual feature. The flag flown here is the thirty-six-star American flag, the one flown at the dedication of the monument over 125 years ago. The inscription on the monument also notes, "It is said that only this monument and Arlington National Cemetery are permitted to fly the American flag at half staff the year round." The Treue der Union Monument is located on High Street, between Third and Fourth Streets (29°58.19'N, 98°59.84'W).[354]

Duff's command was later expanded into the Thirty-third Texas Cavalry; he served on the Texas coast throughout the remainder of the war. Soon after the Nueces affair, Duff was promoted to colonel of the Thirty-third Texas Cavalry. After the war, he was indicted in Kendall County for lynching and later arrested for murder. Duff escaped to Colorado and later fled to England, where he died. A death certificate out of Surrey County, England, lists a James Duff, age seventy-two, as having died on April 16, 1900.[355]

Kerr County Minutemen

Also in February 1861, a company of Kerr County minutemen was formed to protect the frontier against Indian depredations. The muster roll included H.T. Harbour, captain; F.W. Roberts, first lieutenant; M. Hillaire; Robert Martin; Thomas Ingenhuett; T. Taylor; H. Schwethelm; H.M. Burney; H.T. Paul; A. Wilborn; John F. Ochse; J. Tullard; Sam Lane Jr.; P.M. Stanford; and R.H. Burney.[356]

A War Atrocity

While Captain John Lawhorn's Company C of the Frontier Regiment was stationed at Camp Verde in 1863, it was rumored that a small party of supposed bushwhackers was passing through the country en route to Mexico to avoid conscription. There were eight men and one boy in the party, and it became known that they were from Florence, Williamson County. Why they were termed bushwhackers has never been explained, but it is presumed that they had taken part in certain bushwhacking operations and had been forced to leave that section. Nevertheless, the word was carried to Camp Verde, and a troop of twenty-five men under command of Major W.J. Alexander, Company D of the Texas Rangers, immediately started in pursuit. In the pursuing party were a number of men who were well known to the early settlers of Bandera County, but after the close of the war, they all disappeared, some making haste to get out of the country.[357]

The Confederate patrol from Camp Verde intercepted a group of eight well-mounted and well-equipped men from Williamson County about ten miles south of Hondo. Thinking they had nothing to fear, they surrendered their weapons and rode with the soldiers toward Camp Verde to clear things up with the authorities there. As civilians, they were, of course, free to travel. They were relieved of the cash they carried, which collectively amounted to nearly $1,000. This considerable sum may have had something to do with the events that followed.

While they were camped on the trip back to Camp Verde, one or more of the Confederates suggested that the men should be hanged for "evading Confederate service." This pretext might have been accepted by the other soldiers, or it is possible that some of them thought it was just a prank.

Horsehair nooses were made, and if it was a scare, the commanding officer, one Major Anderson, turned a blind eye and did nothing to stop the "prank" once it turned serious. The men were lynched one at a time while the other victims watched and waited their turn.

One man asked to be shot rather than be slowly strangled, and one of the killers complied. The ramrod was left in the musket, and it pierced the man's body, pinning it to the ground. When the bodies were found the next morning, the ramrod was at first mistaken for an arrow, and the killings were thought to be the work of Indians. A boy accompanying the men managed to escape but was never heard from.

After the war, the atrocity was remembered and referred to a tribunal. However, the soldiers had all left Texas, and none, including Major Anderson, could be located for trial. The culprit was W.J. Alexander, major commanding, Southern Division, Mounted Regiment Texas State Troops, Camp Verde.

After completing their work, the men who had participated in this crime (those who refused to have a hand in it having passed on) came to Bandera the next morning and proceeded on to Camp Verde immediately, some of the party hinting to citizens that they had rid the country of some more bushwhackers. Alexander's men had their victims' horses, saddles, bedding, clothing and shoes.

An inquest was held and the verdict rendered as follows: "We the jury, find that these men [giving their names] were killed by Maj. W.J. Alexander's company." A mass grave was dug, and the bodies of the eight unfortunate men were rolled into it and covered up. Many years later, a tombstone was erected over the grave, and on this tombstone appear the names of the men who were murdered while prisoners; the very same men who had been given a sacred pledge that they would be given just treatment if they surrendered. Not one of the men charged in the indictment was ever arrested.

15

Prison Canyon

Some six hundred Union soldiers captured leaving Texas early in the Civil War were locked up in Prison Canyon immediately southwest of Camp Verde (29°53.338′N, 99°7.682′W). This prisoner of war camp featured three cliffs, described as "very difficult to ascend," surrounding the internment area. Prisoners were confined there from September 1861 until August 1862.[358]

Stephan Schwartz

Stephan Schwartz arrived at the Camp Verde prisoner of war camp on September 3, 1861. He spent twenty-two months as a prisoner of war, mostly at Camp Verde. His memoir of imprisonment at the hands of the Confederates provides an intimate and detailed description of daily life at Prison Canyon.[359]

Schwartz enlisted in the United States Army on August 19, 1857. Assigned to Texas, he was in Company I of the First U.S. Infantry. At the time of the outbreak of the Civil War, Schwartz was a hospital steward in San Antonio. The terms of surrender, which General Twiggs negotiated as commander of the U.S. Army's Department of Texas, stated that "all United States troops stationed in New Mexico and Texas, be allowed to leave with the full honors of war, and not to be molested whatsoever on their route." In the West, seven companies of the U.S. Eighth Infantry were posted at Fort Davis, Texas, and Fort Stanton, New Mexico. The Eighth United States Infantry Band was at this time stationed in San Antonio.

Under the command of Lieutenant Colonel Isaac Reeves, the seven companies of the Eighth U.S. Infantry were captured en route to San Antonio. On the long trek east, Reeves's force was reduced by desertion, sickness and drunkenness, its number shrinking from 347 to 270. When the column finally went into camp at San Lucas Spring at the base of Adams's Hill, fifteen miles west of San Antonio, Reeves was confronted by Colonel Earl Van Dorn and 1,370 Texans, most of them mounted and anxious for a fight. Fatigued, outnumbered and intimidated, Reeves surrendered his small force. "I have taken all the U.S. Troops in Texas prisoners of war, and now lean back in my chair and smoke my pipe in peace," crowed Van Dorn, a tough Mississippian. Van Dorn had been an officer with the Second U.S. Cavalry in Texas.[360]

In San Antonio, Schwartz became part of Company C of the Eighth U.S. Infantry. He soon was assigned to the Eighth Infantry Band, which also was among the prisoners of war. Not being a musician, he became the lantern holder at evening concerts, of which there were many in San Antonio. The Eighth Infantry Band (POW) marched in a Fourth of July parade through the main streets of San Antonio out to San Pedro Springs—at that time, three miles from downtown. The band played all the national pieces it knew and some popular "sing songs."[361]

Escorted by twenty men of Captain W.M. Graham's Company, the prisoners were transferred to Camp Verde in September 1861. It was a three-day walk to the new POW camp located about "four to five hundred yards from old Camp Verdee." A company of Confederate soldiers commanded by Captain Dill occupied the old army post at that time. Upon arrival, the prisoners began pitching their tents. They immediately had to strike their tents and turn all of their equipment over to the Confederate quartermaster at Camp Verde. They had to live like wolves for a while, sheltered in dugouts along the cliff walls. Prisoners eventually were able to cobble together shacks using the "wood butcher's art."[362]

> *Our tents were taken away, and we had to make out as best we could. The cold weather was setting in, and we had not too plenty of clothing or blankets; but necessity is the mother of invention; so all hands went to work to build houses for the winter, some in twos and some in fours, just as they*

> *fancied, in partnership, as the labor was too much to do alone, and in an incredibly short time (without tools of any kind) there was quite a town built up, of some one hundred and twenty houses, or shanties, which we called Lincolnville.*[363]

THE SCENE AT PRISON CANYON

Buck Nowlin, interviewed by the *Kerrville Times* in 1994, noted that the name of the POW camp was Prison Canyon. Nowlin recalled, "A building was erected near the confluence of Prison Creek and Verde Creek, near the entrance to the canyon, which is a series of high bluffs. The foundation of the prison, built of native stone, was still evident a few years ago." This foundation now supports the main ranch house at Prison Canyon Ranch.[364]

Surprisingly, there were women in this prisoner of war camp. Schwartz wrote, "There were ten married ladies, having the occupation of laundresses, that belonged to the Band, and different Companies and who were with their husbands in 'Prisontown.'"

Initially, companies from the Third Texas Infantry guarded the POWs early in the war. Later, command of the POW camp devolved to Captain Stokely M. Holmes of Wood's Regiment, Thirty-second Texas Cavalry. Stephan Schwartz describes Holmes as a tyrant. The Confederate soldiers in Holmes's command "insulted the prisoners daily and maltreated them with violence by their throwing stones, or brick-bats, etc., at prisoners, if any of us were passing near or through their camp."[365]

This area of the Texas Hill Country was populated by Germans and others who had a strong Unionist sentiment. The Confederate army at Camp Verde and in San Antonio became concerned that these Unionist sympathizers would try to free the prisoners and become a guerrilla force or escape to Mexico to rejoin the U.S. Army. In reaction to a rumor that Unionist men were hiding near Prison Canyon, sentries were posted at close intervals, citizens were forbidden to enter and conversations with civilians at the camp perimeter were forbidden.[366]

Ultimately, the Union prisoners dispersed from Prison Canyon. After three months and fifteen days at Camp Verde, six companies of the Eighth Infantry—some 330 men—were marched out of Camp Verde on December 4, 1861, to be distributed as follows:

One company to Fort McKavett
One company to Fort Mason
One company to Camp Colorado
Two companies to Fort Chadbourne
One company to Camp Cooper

Only Company C of the Eighth U.S. Infantry and the band remained at the Prison Canyon POW Camp. Sixty men had the place to themselves. They wasted little time in picking out the best shacks from among those vacated the day before. On Christmas Eve 1861, the prisoners had a large party, followed by a parade through the camp. With the band at the head of the procession, followed by the wives and laundresses and then followed by the soldiers of Company C, the parade marched proudly through the streets of Prison Canyon. The band stepped off with "Yankee Doodle," marching by twos and playing all the national pieces it could remember. There were retributions: no more music.[367]

Finding themselves in desperate need of clothing, the prisoners pleaded for something to replace their rags. Shortly after, each prisoner received the following articles of clothing:

One pair of striped homemade trousers
Two pairs of cotton stockings
Two pairs of drawers
One striped duster
One old "stovepipe" hat
One pair of boots[368]

The scattered companies of the Eighth U.S. Infantry returned to Camp Verde and Prison Canyon in early July 1862. Two weeks later, all the prisoners were marched about sixty miles to San Antonio Springs and later imprisoned at San Pedro Springs. Finally paroled on January 2, 1863, these 278 prisoners of war began their long journey home.

Today, the POW camp is located at Prison Canyon Ranch. Unfortunately, the steep-walled canyon was dammed, and the old prison compound lies beneath lake water. This historical site is not registered, is not accessible to the public and is not marked by any historical commemorative inscription.

16

Frontier Regiment and Organization

Frontier Regiment

The Frontier Regiment is the name history has given to a regiment of rangers authorized by the Ninth Legislature of Texas on December 21, 1861, for the protection of the northern and western frontier of Texas. Detachments of at least twenty-five men each were stationed twenty-five miles apart and just west of the line of settlement from the Red River to the Rio Grande. The act and the raising of the regiment were the state's political and military response to the vulnerabilities posed to the state's frontier settlements by the planned withdrawal and redeployment of the Confederate First Regiment, Texas Mounted Riflemen, from its frontier forts.[369] Camp Verde was one of the Red River–Rio Grande line of posts a day's ride apart. The troops furnished their own guns and mounts but often lacked food, clothing and supplies. Still, scouting parties and patrols blunted hostile raids until war's end.[370]

A second Camp Verde, located two miles below (downstream) old Camp Verde in Kerr County, was established on March 31, 1862, by James M. Norris as a ranger station for the Frontier Regiment. This site is known today as Camp Verde, CSA, and is not the site of the original U.S. Army post of Camp Verde, USA. Camp Verde, CSA, was located on today's Verde Creek Road, approximately one mile east of the Camp Verde Store, near the crossing of Verde Creek, at Dr. James Crispin Nowlin's old house.[371] This site was located on what would later become the location of the Camp Verde schoolhouse (29°53.816'N, 99°5.671'W).[372] It was garrisoned by members of Charles S. DeMontel's Company and served as a frontier outpost, probably until the consolidation of the regiment in March 1864.

This second Camp Verde was designated as the headquarters of the Southern Ranging District, commanded by Colonel James E. McCord in 1862 and 1863. McCord abandoned the passive patrol system begun by Norris and instituted a series of aggressive actions against the Indian raiding parties. With McCord in command, the Frontier Regiment saw its greatest success during the summer and fall of 1863.[373] The Frontier Regiment became Texas State Troops in 1862, later becoming the Thirty-sixth Texas Cavalry in the Confederate service in 1864. The transfer spelled the effective end of Texas's Frontier Regiment. Within weeks of the transfer, most of the ranger companies composing the Frontier Regiment had been stripped from the frontier and redeployed to other areas. Company D of the Texas Rangers, commanded by Captain Charles S. DeMontel, was stationed at Camp Verde in March 1862. In May 1863, command was transferred to Major W.J. Alexander until May 1864.[374]

At Camp Verde, CSA, Captain John Lawhorn commanded Company C of the Frontier Regiment from May 1863 through March 1864. This unit may also have been designated as Company B. Company K was at Camp Verde in January 1864, under the command of Captain William G. O'Brian. Company I, under the command of Captain James J. Callan, was at Camp Verde in March 1864. Captain Callan was reported as a deserter.[375]

The Mounted Regiment, Texas State Troops, was transferred into the Confederate army on March 1, 1864. The transfer spelled the effective end of Texas's Frontier Regiment. While not very successful in its mission, it had, nonetheless, provided a measure of effective reassurance to Texas's frontier communities at a time of terror.

On March 31, 1864, several anxious families of Gillespie, Kerr and Kendall Counties—already victimized by both jayhawkers[376] and Indians—"forted up" together in common defense. Upon hearing that Company A at Camp Davis in Gillespie County had been redeployed, they petitioned the adjutant general to block the move.[377]

They were unsuccessful. On April 11, 1864, McCord himself was ordered to concentrate what was left of his regiment in Austin and then to proceed with it to Anderson in Grimes County in east Texas. Challenged by two simultaneous wars, the frontier settlers within a few short weeks were conjoined with and then abandoned by the Confederacy. The dire situation on the Texas frontier in 1864 might have gotten worse had it not been for another state military initiative: the Frontier Organization.

FRONTIER ORGANIZATION

The Frontier Organization represented the final modification of frontier defense in Texas during the Civil War. The law, which established the Frontier Organization and transferred the Frontier Regiment, passed the legislature on December 15, 1863. The law declared that all persons liable for military service who were actual residents of the frontier counties of Texas were to be enrolled into companies of from twenty-five to sixty-five men.

In January 1864, Governor Murrah appointed three men to take command of the frontier districts. William Quayle commanded the First Frontier District, headquartered in Decatur; George Bernard Erath commanded the Second Frontier District, headquartered in Gatesville; and James M. Hunter commanded the Third Frontier District, headquartered in Fredericksburg. The Third Frontier District included Camp Verde. Nearly four thousand men were on the rolls of the organization by the time of the Frontier Regiment's transfer on March 1, 1864.[378]

DIRE STRAITS IN THE VERDE VALLEY

The situation in the Verde Valley grew steadily horrific, as evidenced by an 1864 letter from E.M. Downs of Hondo to Colonel A.G. Dickson.[379] Downs wrote:

> *Within two weeks, and since the removal of the troops from Camp Verde, the Indians have made two visits to this neighborhood, killed two good, loyal citizens, killed and driven off nearly all our horses. We are now not only exposed to the depredations of the Indians, but our worse foe, the renegades and organized members of the Union League. We have very little confidence*

> *in the present partially organized troops of the frontier, as we believe many of them are men that have fled from the interior to avoid conscription and are and have been Union men from the first, and are friends and sympathizers with the deserters and renegades that infest the mountains of this frontier and the Rio Grande.*

The frontier at Camp Verde was becoming untenable for settlers. Civilization, as they knew it, unraveled. Overrun by Indians, army deserters, outlaws and bushwhackers, the pioneers reverted to the old rough-and-ready frontiersman character, forming their own vigilante forces to protect their lives, their loved ones and their property. This was a desperate time, calling forth ordinary citizens to perform extraordinary feats of bravery.

17

Camp Verde, USA, Reactivated

General Robert E. Lee surrendered on April 9, 1865. On April 12, a formal ceremony marked the disbandment of the Army of Northern Virginia and the parole of its officers and men, effectively ending the war in Virginia. The Civil War had ended.

Kerr County Was the Frontier, and Outlaws Besieged the Countryside

Armed bands of highwaymen began to commit depredations, and lawlessness increased throughout the state. When the last vestige of Confederate authority vanished with the surrender of the department by Smith and Magruder, wild rumors circulated picturing the punishment that would be inflicted on those who had taken any prominent part in the affairs of the state or the Confederacy. Many became panic-stricken, and others declared they would not live under the rule of the Yankees. An exodus commenced across the border into Mexico. The high officials of the state, including Governor Murrah himself, were among those who fled. Former Governor Clark, General Smith, General Magruder and many others followed their example. Government disappeared entirely, and by the time General Gordon Granger landed at Galveston with a force of Federal troops on June 19, bedlam was pervasive.[380]

At the end of the war, nearly five thousand Texans had deserted from Confederate and state service, and an unknown number avoided conscription. Formal order had disappeared into lawlessness in many areas of Texas. Camp Verde and Camp Ives had been abandoned at war's end. Local minutemen and vigilantes patrolled the county and stood guard at Bandera Pass. Their duty was to intercept brigands, rustlers, fugitives and hell-raisers who were taking advantage of the breakdown of law and order in this rough area. The number of outlaws in Kerr County swelled to hundreds. Most outlaws were army veterans, proficient, well-armed and wretched gunmen of the outlaw Josey Wales's sort.[381]

The Comanche, Kiowa, Lipan Apache and Kickapoo Indian nations were determined to retain the lands they had taken back during the Civil War. The Indian tribes had become aggressive during the absence of military forces from the Hill Country during the war. Hostile Indian warriors pushed back the frontier fifty miles or more. There is no question that settlers suffered greatly, having perhaps four hundred men, women and children killed, wounded or carried off along the edge of western civilization in Texas.[382] The frontier west of the Gainesville-Fredericksburg-Kerrville line was abandoned by all but a few brave people who moved into stockades. "The worst raids were on moonlit nights, and the soft summer moon became a harbinger of death."[383]

Farther west, the Ninth Cavalry (Buffalo Soldiers) was under constant duress in west Texas, where it fought for eight long, miserable years.[384] The regiment was spread out between Fort Davis in the Davis Mountains and Fort Stockton at Comanche Springs, directly on the Comanche war trail. Raids were nearly constant. In December 1867, a combined force of nearly one thousand Lipans and Kickapoos, accompanied by renegade whites and Mexicans, carried out a vicious attack on a company of Ninth Cavalry troopers. Twenty Indians and three Buffalo Soldiers were killed.[385]

Kickapoo Indians

A new fearsome Indian nation appeared in the Texas Hill Country. These were the Kickapoos. The Kickapoo Nation's long and arduous migration from Illinois to Texas is a complex story of treaties, land cessions and reservation divisions. The Kickapoos were initially invited to settle in

Texas by Spanish colonial officials, who hoped to use displaced Indians as a buffer against American expansion. In 1849, the Mexican government offered land in eastern Coahuila to Kickapoos willing to settle and fight the Comanches and Apaches. One band of Kickapoos under Papiquan accepted and moved south in 1850.[386]

In Mexico, the Kickapoos made trouble for Texans by allying themselves with the Mexican military, serving their new country as raiders into Texas and as border sentinels. Kickapoos, operating out of Morelos, Coahuila—with Caddo, Cherokee, Delaware and Seminole partners—harassed settlements in South Texas while successfully repelling Comanche and Apache encroachments from the north. In return for this service, the Mexican government awarded the tribe 78,000 acres of land near Zaragoza and Remolino. In 1852, the tribe traded this grant for 17,352 acres at El Nacimiento (28°4′N, 101°39′W) and an equal amount in Durango that the tribe never occupied. This El Nacimiento grant established a permanent Kickapoo presence in northern Mexico, and the settlement remains home to most of today's Kickapoos.[387]

The Oklahoma Kickapoos decided to join their relatives in northern Mexico, but while crossing Texas in 1865, they were attacked by Confederate cavalry. The Texas state troops of James Ebenezer McCord's Regiment mistook them for a Comanche-Kiowa band that was raiding Texan settlements. In the battle, the five hundred Texans moved to flush the band from the woods and found a very large group of Kickapoos, several hundred in number. It was the largest fight with Indians during the Civil War, and the Indians won it. This battle was known as the Battle of Dove Creek. It took place on January 8, 1865, at the confluence of Dove Creek and the Concho River in present Tom Green County, some twenty miles southwest of the site of present San Angelo.[388]

Mexican Kickapoos raided southern Texas afterward in retaliation. These raids continued after the Civil War. Attacks intensified from occasional skirmishes to full-scale raids into central Texas north of the Nueces River, including the Camp Verde area. Kickapoo raiders found they could easily elude army pursuit by crossing the Rio Grande back into Mexico.

The Mexican Kickapoos who stayed in Mexico were given a seventeen-thousand-acre reservation in the Santa Rosa Mountains of Coahuila by the Mexican government. The Mexican Kickapoos have remained in Coahuila ever since then. The Kickapoos have traditionally camped near the international bridge between Piedras Negras, Coahuila, and Eagle Pass, Texas.[389]

On January 8, 1983, Public Law 97–429 resolved the Kickapoos' ambiguous land situation. Under this statute, they were officially granted lands near El Indio, Texas, and became identified by United States authorities as the Texas Band of the Oklahoma Kickapoos, thereby becoming eligible for federal aid. Nevertheless, the people still call themselves the Mexican Kickapoos, as they are called in Mexico, their primary place of residence.

The group, which numbers between 625 and 650, spends the major portion of the year in El Nacimiento—about 130 miles southwest of Eagle Pass, Texas. Eight miles south of Eagle Pass is El Indio, the 125-acre reservation for the Kickapoo Indians. The tribe operates the Lucky Eagle Casino, the only land-based casino in the state of Texas.[390]

Fourth U.S. Cavalry

Federal troops did not arrive in Texas to restore order until June 19, 1865, when Union major general Gordon Granger and two thousand Union soldiers arrived on Galveston Island to take possession of the state and enforce slaves' new freedoms. The Texas holiday Juneteenth commemorates this date. The Stars and Stripes were not raised over Austin until June 25, 1865.[391]

Comanches, Kiowas, Lipan Apaches and Kickapoos controlled the Hill Country above the Balcones Escarpment. The Fourth U.S. Cavalry was ordered into Texas in 1866 to combat these tough adversaries. The regiment was filled with skilled Civil War veterans from both armies and outfitted with the latest and best equipment. In War Department records of that day, the Fourth Cavalry was rated the best cavalry regiment in the U.S. Army. Ten companies were concentrated at San Antonio, and two companies were sent to the Rio Grande. In the fall of 1866, companies were sent to Camp Verde, old Fort Martin Scott at Fredericksburg and Fort Mason.[392]

Samuel P. Heintzelman, now a major general, returned to Camp Verde in October 1866, accompanied by his old friends Samuel Maverick and Poli Rodríguez. Heintzelman found the post largely deserted and little more than a "cattle rancho." Only an Irish family was living at the post, and most of the structures were dilapidated. The fences, sutler's store[393] and other buildings had simply disappeared.[394]

Camp Verde was repaired and reopened in 1866 and garrisoned by troopers of the Fourth U.S. Cavalry. Major J.P. Hatch commanded

Soldiers in Bandera Pass. *Photo by Bryden Starr.*

Companies B and L at Camp Verde. The troopers began active patrolling from Camp Verde while making improvements to the garrison. Cavalry patrols were continuously in the field. These extensive sorties were made through the watersheds of the Pecos, Nueces, Frio, Medina, Guadalupe, Llano and Pedernales Rivers. A number of skirmishes were fought with the Kickapoos in Kerr County and the surrounding Hill Country.[395]

The post return for November 1866 indicates the following disposition:

C.S. Bowman, Capt. and Bvt. Major, Fourth Cav., commanding Company L.

Post returns for April 1867 list the following:

John P. Hatch, Major and Bvt. Brigadier General, Commanding Post and Fourth U.S. Cavalry.
Wirt Davis, Captain Bvt. Major, Fourth U.S. Cavalry
Charles S. Bowman, Capt. Bvt. Major, Fourth U.S. Cavalry. Commanding Company L.
George S. Huntt, Capt. Fourth U.S. Cavalry, Commanding Company H.
Clarence Mauck, Capt. Bvt. Major, Fourth U.S. Cavalry. Commanding Company B

Miles Keogh was assigned to this unit and post but was absent with leave and never served at Camp Verde. Camp Verde Post Returns for 1868 record the following actions:[396]

George C. Cram, Major, Commanding Officer of Post and Commanding Fourth U.S. Cavalry Regiment.

Clarence Mauck, Commanding Company B.

Oliver Grosvenor, Commanding Company L.

Capt. Charles S. Bowman died at Camp Verde on January 3, 1868.[397]

January 4 to 7, 1868: Sgt W. Stewart, Fourth Cavalry from Camp Verde, Texas. Troops from Fourth Cavalry {Cos B & L}. Thirteen men passed through country through Medina River. Traveled 80 miles to operate against the Kickapoo.

February 4 to 6, 1868: Second Lt. O. Grosvenor, Fourth Cavalry from Camp Verde, Texas, Troops from Fourth Cavalry {Cos B & L} one officer/18 men. Passed through country along Rio Guadalupe. Traveled a distance of 90 miles against the Kickapoo Indians.

February 6 to 10, 1868: Second Lt J.M. Walton, Fourth Cavalry from Camp Verde, Texas. Troops from Fourth Cavalry {Cos B & L} one officer/26 men. Passed through Medina River. Traveled a distance of 120 miles to operate against Kickapoo Indians.

February 7 to 9, 1868: Corporal J. Mauley, Fourth Cavalry from Camp Verde, Texas. Troops from Fourth Cavalry {Cos. B & L} Six men. Passed through Guadalupe and Pedernales rivers; traveled a distance of 80 miles to operate against the Kickapoo Indians.

March 1 to 4, 1868: First Lt. William J. Maberly, Fourth Cavalry from Camp Verde Texas. Troops from Fourth Cavalry {Cos B & L} One officer/17 men passed through country Rio Pecos and Rio Hondo; traveled a distance of 125 miles to operate against Kickapoo Indians. Abundant signs seen.[398]

Thomas Clark was killed by Indians above Bandera in 1866. David Cryer was killed that year ten miles north of Bandera. Thomas Click was also killed by Indians in 1866, on the Medina River above Bandera. Samuel Love was killed two miles above Kerrville. B. Shack was killed by Indians in 1866 on the Medina above Bandera.[399]

FIFTH UNITED STATES INFANTRY

In 1868, Camp Verde was garrisoned by Company C of the Fifth United States Infantry. It was part of the troops assigned to the Fifth Military District, commanded by Brevet Major General E.R.S. Canby.[400]

THIRTY-FIFTH UNITED STATES INFANTRY

By 1868, Camp Verde was occupied by the Thirty-fifth Infantry, consisting of one company commanded by Captain H.A. Ellis. Troops arrived at Camp Verde on March 17, 1868. Companies L and I left on April 9, 1868, and arrived at Fort McKavett on April 21, 1868.

These were the last soldiers assigned to Camp Verde.

CAMP VERDE, USA, IS CLOSED

Finally, the military role of Camp Verde ended on April 1, 1869, when the U.S. Army post was closed. The Fourth Cavalry was subsequently concentrated in large garrisons, including San Antonio, Fort Concho, Fort Duncan, Fort Griffin, Fort McKavett and Fort Clark.[401]

By the early 1870s, Kickapoo depredations had become such a serious problem that many Texans called on the cavalry to violate the international border and subdue the offending Indians. In 1870, Indians murdered the elderly Mrs. Vance, and her body was thrown into Verde Creek.[402]

Although Camp Verde had been abandoned, the Fourth Cavalry continued to operate in the Hill Country. On July 4, 1871, Company M of the Fourth Cavalry fought a skirmish in Bandera Pass. Sergeant D. Harrington, with ten troopers, left San Antonio on June 27, 1871, to scout into the Verde Valley area. The troopers came across a band of Indians who were driving a herd of stolen horses through Bandera Pass. In the ensuing engagement, two Indians were wounded, and forty-seven horses were recaptured.

This may well have been the last battle at Bandera Pass.

In November 1873, a full company of the Fourth Cavalry took up a post in Kerrville to deal with the significant increase in lawlessness and Indian raids. These troopers remained in Kerrville until local militia, minutemen and lawmen were able to maintain the peace.[403]

The Freedmen's Bureau at Camp Verde

Camp Verde army post served as the site for the Freedmen's Bureau in Kerr County. The Freedmen's Bureau was an agency of the United States Army.

On June 19 (Juneteenth), 1865, Union general Gordon Granger read the Emancipation Proclamation in Galveston, thus belatedly bringing about the freeing of 250,000 slaves in Texas. The tidings of freedom reached slaves gradually as individual plantation owners read the proclamation to their bondsmen over the months following the end of the war.

The formation of the Bureau of Refugees, Freedmen and Abandoned Lands (Freedmen's Bureau.) presented a threat to Texas antebellum society. The bureau began its operations in the state in September 1865 under the command of Major General Edgar M. Gregory. The bureau was charged with overseeing all matters concerning refugees, freedmen and abandoned lands, but its principal role was helping the new freedmen make the transition from slavery to freedom. Gregory, an abolitionist, interpreted his chief goal in the state as establishing a free labor system for the former slaves. The Freedmen's Bureau was established by Congress in March 1865 as a branch of the United States Army. It was to be a temporary agency. Its functions were to provide relief to the thousands of refugees, black and white, who had been left homeless by the Civil War; to supervise affairs related to newly freed slaves in the Southern states; and to administer all land abandoned by Confederates or confiscated from them during the war.[404]

The Freedmen's Bureau operated in Texas from late September 1865 until July 1870. Between September 1865 and May 1866, when he was relieved, Gregory placed sub-assistant commissioners in stations across east Texas. By May 1, 1866, he had established branches of the bureau in thirty counties, staffed by thirty-one sub-assistant commissioners.[405]

Since Texas was occupied by Union forces rather late in the Civil War and had no "abandoned lands," the bureau in the state was supported at first by the sale and rental of former Confederate government property. Because the Freedmen's Bureau was an agency of the United States Army, Texans generally viewed it as an extension of the army of occupation imposed on them by the victorious North, as further evidence of the Northern desire for revenge.

By the First Reconstruction Act of March 2, 1867, the United States Congress divided the defeated South, already restored under presidential Reconstruction, into five military districts, of which Louisiana and Texas, under General Philip H. Sheridan at New Orleans, constituted the Fifth

Military District. For readmission to the Union under the congressional plan, each unreconstructed state was required to ratify the Fourteenth Amendment and elect by universal manhood suffrage (excluding prewar officeholders who had served the Confederacy) a convention to write a constitution acceptable both to the state's voters and Congress. Sheridan, who was an advocate for freedmen, severely limited voter registration for former Confederates. General Sheridan selected General Charles Griffin as his subordinate in Texas.

Griffin ordered that every commander of troops in an area where no bureau existed act as an agent of the bureau. Therefore, some of the men officially designated as sub-assistant commissioners were stationed at places such as Fort Inge, Camp Verde and Fort Belknap, where there were few or no freedmen.[406]

TEXAS READMITTED TO THE UNION

On February 8, 1870, the elected members of the Twelfth Legislature assembled at Austin at the order of the military commander. They were to adopt the Fourteenth and Fifteenth Amendments and select United States senators in preparation for readmission to the Union. They quickly approved the amendments and selected Morgan C. Hamilton for a six-year term and James W. Flanagan for a four-year term. This completed the requirements set by Congress for readmission. On March 30, 1870, President Grant signed the act that readmitted Texas to the Union and ended congressional Reconstruction.[407]

That year, 1870, Mrs. Wanz, the mother of Xavier Wanz, was killed by Indians on Verde Creek. Also killed on Verde Creek that year were Walter Reese and Mrs. Wallace.[408]

18

The Texas Militia

It was in 1870 that the militia in Texas again began to take form through the organization of volunteer companies authorized by the Militia Bill of that year. The excitement over this bill was intense. It was a stringent law for the organization and drilling of the militia, which was divided into two classes: the state guard, to be composed of volunteer companies, and the reserve military, which included all males subject to military duty not enrolled in volunteer companies.[409]

Kerr County's Company I

In Kerr County, Company I of the Fourteenth Reserve Militia operated in the Camp Verde area. Commanded by Captain Alonzo Rees, the militia company was active in 1870 and 1871.

The state guard and reserve militia of the Reconstruction era were merged into a simple state militia by the Thirteenth Texas Legislature on March 19, 1873. Although clear enabling legislation cannot be found for the next sixteen years, there is reference to "Volunteer Units" in the adjutant general's biennial report of 1876, to officers of the "militia and state troops" in 1878 and to "Texas Volunteer Guards" in 1880.[410]

KERR COUNTY MINUTEMEN

After the ranging companies were mustered out in 1871, Texas was for several months without any form of state protection. However, on November 25, 1871, the second session of the Twelfth Legislature passed an act providing for twenty-four companies of minutemen, who would be enlisted for one year, to continue the protection of the border settlements. This service was limited from the start, however, for the act stipulated that the time of employment in the field should not exceed ten days a month.

Each company was to consist of one lieutenant elected by the members, two sergeants, two corporals and fifteen men. Company recruits were required to be citizens of the county in which the unit was located or of the adjoining county, and they had to provide their own horses. Salary was to be two dollars a day while in actual service; this money was to come out of the cash received by the governor from the hypothecation of frontier defense bonds. However, before the governor could use any of it for the minutemen, he was required to pay off the ranger companies.

Lieutenant Henry Schwethelm commanded Company E of the Kerr County Volunteer Minutemen at Camp Verde from 1873 to 1878.[411]

Kerr County continued to be plagued by outlaws through the 1870s. In July 1873, a gang of seventeen outlaws attempted to rob the store of Valentine and Schreiner in Kerrville. Forewarned, the owners killed five of the outlaws, but twelve escaped. A posse of eight men caught these outlaws about ten miles from Kerrville and apparently killed all but a very few.[412]

In August 1873, another gang was captured near Buffalo Branch, which leads into the south fork of the Guadalupe River, about twenty miles above Kerrville (29°59.943′N, 99°23.021′W). Nearby caves yielded a harvest of Native American goods, including lances, bows, arrows, masks and war paint. It seems that much of the Indian raiding had been the work of this gang of fifty to sixty white men posing as Indians. They were responsible for the killing of Mrs. Joseph Moore and children, as well as the killing of Mr. Alexander.

W.B. Terry and two children were killed by Indians in 1876, ten miles below Kerrville at the mouth of Verde Creek.

The last raid by Lipan Apaches in Frio Canyon occurred on April 19, 1881, with the killing of Katherine McLauren and a neighbor boy, Allen Lease.[413] Lieutenant Bullis chased the Indians into Mexico and oblivion. The frontier was fast disappearing. Nevertheless, the need for defense endured.

Kerrville Mountaineers

The continued Indian menace caused a home guard unit—the Kerrville Mounted Rifles—to be organized in 1875, and Charles A. Schreiner was elected captain, a title he carried the rest of his life. These mountaineers fought a battle with horse thieves in 1876 at Flat Rock at the head of the Pedernales River in Kerr County. Among the men from Kerrville were Charles Schreiner, Robert Jarmon, Jones Glenn, Ralph Bacon, Jim Pruitt, Hiram Davis, Jim Holloman and F.J. Hamer.[414]

19
The Frontier Battalion

Beginning in 1870, Texans resolved to solve their own problems through the Texas Ranger Frontier Forces. The legislature passed a series of acts authorizing county-based ranger companies of 25 to 75 men "for each county that may be so infested" with "marauding or thieving parties." If this proved ineffective, the governor was authorized to raise a battalion of up to 450 mounted men in six companies of up to 75 men each. If this still was inadequate, the governor could call out unlimited numbers of volunteer minutemen.

Because of expenses, the companies of the Frontier Forces were from time to time consolidated, until the force comprised seven companies, which were finally mustered out on May 31 and June 15, 1871.[415]

The place of the Frontier Forces was taken in 1874 by the Frontier Battalion, organized by an act passed on April 10, 1874. During the first seventeen months of its organization, the battalion had twenty-one fights with Indians; from September 1875 to February 1876, no Indians appeared on the border guarded by the battalion, and a new feeling of security resulted.

The Frontier Battalion was reorganized as the Ranger Force by an act of the Twenty-seventh Texas Legislature on March 29, 1901. From time to time, this regular force was supplemented by specially commissioned Special Rangers, Railroad Rangers, Cattlemen's Association Rangers and Loyalty Rangers. Finally, on August 10, 1935, the Ranger Force was transferred to the Texas Department of Public Safety.

John W. Sansom

Captain John W. Sansom commanded Company C, Frontier Forces, at the lower Camp Verde in 1870 and 1871.[416] Company C included a lieutenant, a medical officer, four corporals, a farrier, a bugler and fifty privates. The men occupied twenty tents, and the officers operated out of an old house owned by Dr. James Crispin Nowlin, the company medical officer.[417]

The Company Roster for Company C in 1871 included the following:[418]

John W. Sansom, Captain
James C. Nowlin, Medical Officer
Charles A. Patton, Lieutenant

Abstract 11 — Voucher 49 — Aug to Dec 1871 — [illegible]

Final Statement of James C Nowlin a Surgeon of Capt. John W Sansom Company ("C") of the Frontier Forces, born in Coldwell Co. in the State of Kentucky, aged 54 years 6 feet 3 inches high, dark complexion, dark eyes, dark hair, and by occupation a Surgeon, was mustered into service by Ira H Evans, at Austin, on the 25th day of Aug. 1870, to serve for 12 months, unless sooner discharged, who is now entitled to a discharge by reason of Special Orders No. 46, from the Governor.

The said James C Nowlin has never been paid.

He has pay due him from Aug. 25th 1870 to May 31st 1871.

~~He is indebted to the State of Texas for one Winchester carbine, and to~~

I Certify that the above Final Statement, given in duplicate at Fort Griffin, this 31st day of May 1871, is correct.

John W Sansom
Capt Co. "C" F F Commanding Co.

I Certify that the above Final Statement of James C Nowlin Co. "C", Frontier Forces, is a true and correct copy of the original, filed in the Comptroller's office of the State of Texas.

W. H. King Adj. Genl

James C. Nowlin, MD.
Texas Frontier Service Certificate.

NEIL COLDWELL

Captain Neil Coldwell of Center Point was the commander of Company F of the Frontier Battalion. Pat Dolan was his first lieutenant, and F.W. Nelson was the second lieutenant. Coldwell served nearly ten years as a ranger, while most rangers lasted at best a year or two.[419]

Captain Coldwell served gallantly throughout the Civil War in the Thirty-second Regiment, Texas Cavalry, commanded by Colonel W.P. Woods. At the organization of the Frontier Battalion in 1874, he was commissioned captain of Company F. The station of Company F was the most inhospitable of the lot. Company F was stationed on Contrary Creek (30°10.007′N, 99°22.332′W) in far western Kerr County; Coldwell's territory included the heads of the Guadalupe, Nueces, Llano and Devil's Rivers, the roughest and most difficult part of southern Texas.[420]

In 1879, Coldwell was designated quartermaster of the Frontier Battalion. In 1883, his service on the frontier came to an end. During his career, he fought many victorious skirmishes with Indians and outlaws.

Conclusion

Camp Verde Ranch

Captain John A. Bonnell, a retired Union officer, purchased 640 acres where the old buildings of Camp Verde stood in 1874. His son, Will H. Bonnell, added 20,000 acres, and the land was used for a stock ranch. Will H. Bonnell and his family occupied the building made for officers' quarters until 1929, when the ranch was sold to Walter and Richard Nowlin.[421] They were relatives of Dr. James Crispin Nowlin, a Texas Ranger at Camp Verde.

During the cholera scare of 1892, General Wheaton, who was in command of the Department of Texas, sent some officers to Camp Verde who took an option lease on the property for a year, with a privilege of longer time, so they could absolutely have a quarantine camp by closing roads and stopping all travel to this place.

In the *Kerrville Mountain Sun* of April 2, 1910, there is an account of the fire at Camp Verde on March 26, 1910. Owners were Captain and Judge W.H. Bonnell and his wife. Thomas Blair from Hamilton, Ohio, was burned to death in this fire. Ben Lackey was then the ranch foreman and burned his boots before he escaped the fire.

The former officers' quarters building is all that is left of the buildings at Camp Verde. Today, it is used as a residence by the Bowman family. Although this building was severely damaged by the fire in 1910, the sturdy thirty-inch-thick, 13-foot-high walls withstood the blaze, and the structure was rebuilt as an exact replica of the original officers' quarters. The structure faces Verde Creek to the south and measures 110 feet along its front. A north wing extending to the north is 85 feet in length. Nowlin family records indicate that the northeast room was set aside for General Albert Sidney Johnson when he visited Camp Verde. An adjoining room was reserved for Robert E. Lee.[422]

CENTER POINT CEMETERY

Thirty-two Texas Rangers are buried in the Center Point Cemetery, on FM 480 east of Camp Verde (29°56.083'N, 99°2.322'W). Texas Historical Marker #786 honors these rangers: W.D.C. Burney, N. Coldwell, J.A. Gibbens, H.T. Hill, F.L. Holloway, R.J. Irving Sr., J.H. Lane, S.T. Lane Jr., T. Lane, R.J. Lange, M.A. Lowrance, J.L. McElroy, S.G. McElroy, A.S. Moore, F.M. Moore, G.K. Moore, G.R. Moore, G.W. Moore, H.C. Moore, James Moore, J.T. Moore, M.F. Moore, J.C. Nowlin, R.W. Nowlin, P. Alonzo Rees, N.O. Reynolds, W.H. Rishworth, J.L. Sellars, A.J. Sowell, W.H. Witt and S.G. Wray.

HISTORIC CAMP VERDE STORE

The celebrated Camp Verde General Store is located at what may be the most historic crossroads in Kerr County (29°53.678'N, 99°6.419'W). From this storied place, visitors can look out upon the frontier of the Verde Valley that has been the setting for the play of historic events for hundreds of years.

The Camp Verde Store is situated on the north bank of Verde Creek six miles southwest of Center Point in southeastern Kerr County. It grew around the Williams community store, established adjacent to Camp Verde in 1857 in order to serve the needs of soldiers stationed there. It is reported that the primary purpose of the store was to provide liquor to the soldiers because regulations prohibited the sale of intoxicants within the camp. John Williams's store was located about one hundred yards west of the present-day store, now at the intersection of Highway 173 and East Verde Creek Road.[423]

When John Williams's health failed in 1858,[424] the store was acquired by Charles A. Schreiner, then a young rancher in the nearby Turtle Creek area who had recently emigrated from Germany. Since the store was open only on

Above: Camp Verde Store. *Photo by author.*

Left: Penateka Marker, dedicated 2011 by former Texas Ranger Joe Davis and Johnny Wauqua, chairman, Comanche Indian tribe. *Photo by author.*

army paydays, Schreiner and his brother-in-law, Caspar Real, supplemented the business by contracting with the federal government to supply wood and beef to the military post.[425]

A post office and store continued to provide irregular service to area inhabitants after the military camp was abandoned. Camp Verde's first post office was established in 1858, probably operated from Schreiner's store. It discontinued operation in 1866. Charles C. Kelley served as postmaster when the post office was reopened at a different location in 1887. In 1892, however, it, too, was closed. Walter S. Nowlin reestablished the store and post office in 1899. Both remain in operation to the present day. The present Camp Verde Store was constructed in 1908 after a flood washed away the original store building.[426]

Since 2003, Camp Verde General Store has been gradually undergoing revitalization, modernizing the store while maintaining the heritage and historic character of the building. Today, the Camp Verde Store is a popular restaurant and boutique shop, as well as a functioning post office. The Camp Verde Historic Park is immediately across the road from the store and features the crossing of Verde Creek by the old Spanish Trail. Texas State Historical Markers celebrate the history of the local area. The old-fashioned veranda of the store overlooks the park and invites visitors to "sit a spell" and enjoy the historic panorama.[427]

Closing the Frontier

The manifestation of the Texas frontier at Camp Verde, as Lucy Lockwood Hazard would say, "affords the setting; it occasions the plot; it offers the theme; it creates the character." It appears that Camp Verde history is an exercise in the definition of Texas.[428]

Camp Verde is a place and a condition where differences met head-on and often resulted in conflict. "Since conflict is a basic ingredient of the frontier in the novel, the story's action of flight, skirmishing, disguise, warfare, etc. literally becomes theme."[429]

The forging of the unique and rugged Texas identity occurred at the Verde Valley margin between the civilization of settlement and the savagery of wilderness. The interesting twist is the question, "Whose frontier?" There were civilizations, each its own, on both sides of the frontier. Each had its own culture, its own beliefs and its own reality.

The image of Texas derives from this multicultural frontier experience. As Frederick Jackson Turner said, this explains the distinctive features of culture and civilization.[430]

The View from the Veranda

This is the place. The old Camp Verde Store is the focal point of these legends. From this vantage point, visitors can look out upon the Verde Valley frontier that has been a part of Texas history for more than ten thousand years. Standing on the veranda of the historic general store, one can scan south across Verde Creek to the grasslands and mountain slopes upon which Prehistoric Indians, Tonkawas, Jumanos, Lipan Apaches and Penateka Comanches lived, hunted and fought. Here the old Comanche Trail passes within feet of the front porch. A few yards to the west are the ancient routes of the Apache Trail and the famous Spanish Trail. Thousands of cattle

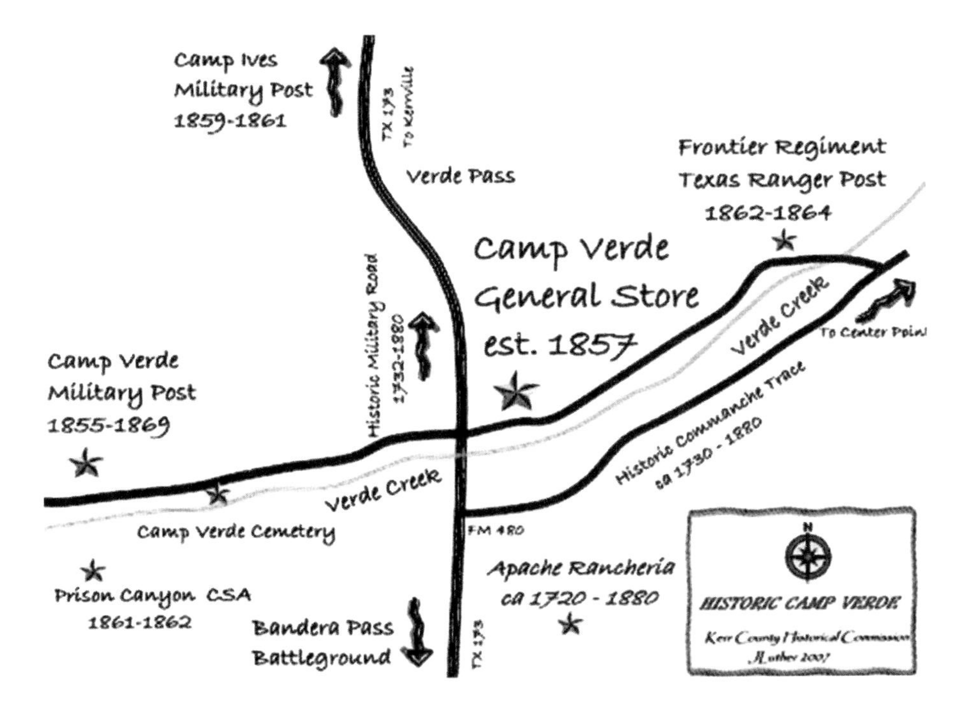

Map of Historic Camp Verde. *Cartography by author.*

once streamed past here on the Great Western Trail. Directly in front of the store is the legendary Verde Creek. Here, Spanish soldiers and missionaries camped while on their expeditions into the wilderness. Beyond the creek on the southern shore is the ancient site of an Apache encampment. To the west is Monte del Mesa, overlooking the old army post and prisoner of war camp. Drums, bugle calls and army band concerts once echoed down this stream. The old Texas Ranger post is a short distance to the east. In the southern prospect is Bandera Pass, the site of desperate battles. The crossroads here is a place of power. Here the frontiersmen of legend rode into our memory and shaped our Texas character.

You wish to see the frontier?
Yes, sir, before it's gone.
—*Dances with Wolves*[431]

Notes

Introduction

1. Karst is a landscape underlain by limestone that has been eroded by dissolution, producing ridges, towers, fissures, sinkholes and other characteristic landforms.
2. E.H. Johnson, "Edwards Plateau," Handbook of Texas Online, http://www.tshaonline.org/handbook/online/articles/rxe01 (accessed November 21, 2011): "The Edwards Plateau, in South Central Texas east of the Pecos River and west of the Colorado, is the southernmost unit of the Great Plains. Physiographically, it is an erosional region with thin soil over beveled Comanchean limestone exposures that extend as limestone beds to constitute the underpinning of the High Plains, lying above the Permian and Triassic beds and beneath the more recent unconsolidated Pliocene and Pleistocene deposits. By and large, however, the Edwards Plateau is erosional with the margins of the region frayed rather deeply so that the plateau as a whole is perceptibly higher than adjacent areas."
3. William Feathergail Wilson, *Hydrogeology of Kerr County* (Bandera, TX: Strata Geological Services, 2008).
4. Ibid.
5. "Pavo Real," *Texas Beyond History*, http://www.texasbeyondhistory.net/pavoreal/site.html (accessed January 15, 2007).

6. Juliana Barr, "Geographies of Power: Mapping Indian Borders in the Borderlands of the Early Southwest," *William and Mary Quarterly* (2011): 68.
7. William Edward Dunn, "Apache Relations in Texas," *Quarterly of the Texas State Historical Association* 4 (July 1910–April 1911): 205.
8. Maria F. Wade, *The Native Americans of the Texas Edwards Plateau, 1582–1799* (Austin: University of Texas Press, 2003), 161.
9. U.S. Army, *Post of Camp Verde, Map No. 15* (Washington, D.C., 1868).
10. *The Last of the Mohicans: A Narrative of 1757* is a historical novel by James Fenimore Cooper, first published in February 1826. It is the second book of the Leatherstocking Tales pentalogy and the best known. *The Pathfinder*, published fourteen years later, in 1840, is its sequel.
11. Lucy Lockwood Hazard, *The Frontier in American Literature* (Boston: Thomas Y. Crowell Company, 1927).
12. Marius Bewley, "James Fenimore Cooper—William Cullen Bryant," in *Major Writers of America*, 2 vols., edited by Perry Miller (New York: Harcourt, Brace & World, 1962).
13. Thomas J. Roundtree, *CliffsNotes on* The Last of the Mohicans, http://www.cliffsnotes.com/study_guide/literature/id-57.html (accessed August 8, 2011).
14. George Bernard Shaw, *Man and Superman*, Act III (Cambridge, MA: The University Press, 1903), 14.
15. Frederick Jackson Turner, "The Significance of the Frontier in American History," scholarly paper read before the American Historical Association in Chicago during the Chicago World's Fair, 1893.
16. Frederick Jackson Turner, *Rise of the New West, 1819–1829*, vol. 14 in the series *American Nation: A History* (n.p., 1906).
17. Sylvia Grider and Lou Rodenberger, "Women and Literature," *Handbook of Texas Online*, http://www.tshaonline.org/handbook/online/articles/kzwcu (accessed November 20, 2011), Texas State Historical Association.
18. Adele Lubbock Briscoe Looscan, "The Women of Pioneer Days," in *A Comprehensive History of Texas: 1685–1845: 1845–1897* (Austin: Texas State Historical Association, 1987).
19. "Verde Creek (Bandera County)," *Handbook of Texas Online*, http://www.tshaonline.org/handbook/online/articles/rbv14 (accessed August 11, 2011), Texas State Historical Association.

CHAPTER 1

20. Timothy K. Perttula, *The Prehistory of Texas* (College Station: Texas A&M University Press, 2004).

21. Ethnohistory uses both historical and ethnographic data as its foundation. Its historical methods and materials go beyond the standard use of documents and manuscripts. Practitioners recognize the utility of such source material as maps, music, paintings, photography, folklore, oral tradition, site exploration, archaeological materials, museum collections, enduring customs, language and place names. *Wikipedia*, http://en.wikipedia.org/wiki/Ethnohistory (accessed 12.12.2011).
22. Thomas R. Hester, Harry J. Shafer and Kenneth L. Feder, *Field Methods in Archeology*, 7th ed. (Palo Alto, CA: Mayfield Publishing Company, 1997).
23. Steve Black, *The Gault Site*, http://www.texasbeyondhistory.net/gault/index.html (accessed December 6, 2011), Texas Beyond History.
24. Chert is fine-grained chalcedonic silica with many aliases, including flint, agate and chalcedony. The dominant characteristic is conchoidal fracture, enabling the handcrafting of tools and projectile points.
25. S. Alan Skinner, "Prehistoric Settlement of the Turtle Creek Watershed: A Preliminary Report," *Texas Archeology* 15, no. 3 (1971): 3–6, 9–13.
26. Joseph H. Labadie, *A Reconnaissance of Electrical Transmission Line Rights-of-Way in Bandera and Kerr Counties, Texas* (San Antonio: Center for Archeological Research, University of Texas, 1987).
27. Thomas R. Hester, *Early Human Populations along the Balcones Escarpment* (San Antonio: Center for Archeological Research, University of Texas at San Antonio), available online at http://www.lib.utexas.edu/geo/balcones_escarpment/pages55-62.html.
28. Ellen Sue Turner, Thomas R. Hester and Richard L. McReynolds, *A Field Guide to Stone Artifacts of Texas Indians* (Lanham, MD: Taylor Trade Publishing, 2011).
29. The Pleistocene is the epoch from 2,588,000 to 11,700 years BP that spans the world's recent period of repeated glaciations.
30. Hester, *Early Human Populations*.
31. Ibid.
32. John Minton, "Real County," *Handbook of Texas Online*, http://www.tshaonline.org/handbook/online/articles/hcr04 (accessed November 20, 2011), Texas State Historical Association.
33. Henry B. Moncure, "An Archeological Survey of the Verde Creek Transmission Line—Kerr County, Texas," *Texas Archeological Survey, Technical Bulletin No. 54* (1981).
34. Brett A. Houck, Kevin A. Miller and Eric R. Oksanen, "The Gatlin Site and the Early-to-Middle Archaic Chronology of the Southern Edwards

Plateau, Texas," *Bulletin of the Texas Archeological Society* 80 (2009); Joseph Luther, "First Peoples on the Upper Guadalupe River," *Kerrville Daily Times*, March 24, 2010.

35. "Atlatl," *Wikipedia*, http://en.wikipedia.org/wiki/Atlatl (accessed December 6, 2011); http://news.nationalgeographic.com/news/2006/01/0124_060124_atlatl_deer.html (accessed December 6, 2011).
36. Moncure, "Archeological Survey."
37. Laurie Moseley, "Indian Cultures during the Late Prehistoric Period," in *Information about Archeology*, Texas Archeological Society (TAS), http://www.txarch.org/archeology/topics/articles/prehistoric.html (accessed December 6, 2011).
38. Nancy Kenmotsu, *Who Were the "Coahuiltecans"? Texas Beyond History*, http://www.texasbeyondhistory.net/st-plains/peoples/coahuiltecans.html (accessed December 6, 2011).
39. Ibid.

CHAPTER 2

40. Michael Collins, "Named Indian Groups in Texas: A Guide to Entries in the New Handbook of Texas," *Bulletin of the Texas Archeological Society* 70 (1999): 7–16.
41. Martha McCullough, *Three Nations, One Place: A Comparative Ethnohistory of Social Change among the Comanches and Hasinais during Spain's Colonial Era, 1689–1821* (New York: Taylor and Francis, Routledge, 2003).
42. David M. Johnson, "Apache Victory against the U.S. Dragoons, the Battle of Cieneguilla, New Mexico," in Douglas Scott, Lawrence Babits and Charles Haecker, *Fields of Conflict: Battlefield Archeology from the Roman Empire to the Korean War* (Westport, CT: Praeger Security International, 2009); Marc Thompson, "A Survey of Aboriginal Metal Points from Apachería," *The Artifact* 18, no. 1 (1980).
43. McCullough, *Three Nations.*
44. Thomas R. Hester, "An Overview of the Archeology of Bandera County, Texas," *La Tierra, Journal of the Southern Texas Archeological Association* 32, no. 2 (2005).
45. Kay E. Hindes, "Historic Camps and Crossings on the Medina and San Antonio Rivers," *Texas Beyond History*, http://www.texasbeyondhistory.net/st-plains/images/he6.html (accessed December 6, 2011); Kay E. Hindes, "Native American and European Contact in the Lower Medina River Valle," *La Tierra* 22, no. 2 (1995): 25–31.

46. Thomas R. Hester, "An Overview of the Archeology of Bandera County, Texas," e-mail communication, 2011.
47. "Coahuiltecan Indian Tribe," http://www.accessgenealogy.com/native/texas/coahuiltecanindianhist.html (accessed February 1, 2007).
48. Randolph Campbell, *Gone to Texas: A History of the Lone Star State* (New York: Oxford University Press, 2003).
49. Herbert E. Bolton, "The Jumano Indians in Texas, 1650–1771," *Quarterly of the Texas State Historical Association* 15, no. 1 (July 1911–April 1912): 66–84.
50. Became part of another old Spanish Trail to San Saba and the west, El Camino Pinta.
51. Thomas Campbell, "Payaya Indians," *Handbook of Texas Online*, http://www.tshaonline.org/handbook/online/articles/bmp53 (accessed April 15, 2011), Texas State Historical Association.
52. *The Tonkawa Indians*, http://www.texasindians.com/tonk.htm (accessed February 1, 2007).
53. Moncure, "Archeological Survey."
54. *Tonkawa Tribal History*, http://www.tonkawatribe.com/history.htm (accessed February 1, 2007).
55. Walter Prescott Webb and H. Bailey Carroll, eds., *The Handbook of Texas* (Austin, 1952), II:789.
56. Light Townsend Cummins and Alvin R. Bailey Jr., eds., *A Guide to the History of Texas* (New York: Greenwood Press, 1988), 94.

CHAPTER 3

57. U.S. Army, *Post of Camp Verde*, Map No. 15, 1865.
58. From 1685 until 1689, a French colony, Fort Saint Louis, existed near what is now Inez, Texas. France did not abandon its claims to Texas until November 3, 1762, when it ceded all of its territory west of the Mississippi River to Spain in the Treaty of Fontainebleau. In 1803, three years after Spain had returned Louisiana to France, Napoleon sold Louisiana to the United States. The original agreement between Spain and France had not explicitly specified the borders of Louisiana, and the descriptions in the documents were ambiguous and contradictory. The United States insisted that its purchase included all of the territory France had claimed, including all of Texas. http://en.wikipedia.org/wiki/French_colonization_of_Texas (accessed November 11, 2011).

59. Curtis D. Tunnell and W.W. Newcomb Jr., *A Lipan Apache Mission, San Lorenzo de la Santa Cruz, 1762–1771* (Bulletin 14 of the Texas Memorial Museum, University of Texas at Austin, 1969), 141.
60. "Encomiendas," *Wikipedia*, http://en.wikipedia.org/wiki/Encomienda (accessed December 6, 2011).
61. Alexander E. Sweet and J. Armoy Knox, *On a Mexican Mustang through Texas, from the Gulf to the Rio Grande* (London: Trubner & Co., 1883), 208.
62. "History of Texas," *Wikipedia*, http://en.wikipedia.org/wiki/History_of_Texas (accessed December 6, 2011).
63. Oakah L. Jones, *Los Paisanos: Spanish Settlers on the Northern Frontier of New Spain* (Norman: University of Oklahoma Press, 1979).
64. Donald E. Chipman, *Spanish Texas, 1519–1821* (Austin: University of Texas Press, 1992).
65. Texas State Historic Marker 5029000096, N29 25.546, W098 29.165.
66. Anne A. Fox and Kristi M. Ulrich, *A Guide to Ceramics from Spanish Colonial Sites in Texas*, Special Report #33 (San Antonio: Center for Archeological Research, University of Texas, 2008), 10–11.
67. Chipman, *Spanish Texas.*
68. Dunn, "Apache Relations," 207.
69. Gerald Betty, *Comanche Society before the Reservation* (College Station: Texas A&M University, 2002), 50–51.
70. Robert Bruce Blake, "Teran De Los Rios, Domingo," *Handbook of Texas Online*, http://www.tshaonline.org/handbook/online/articles/fte13 (accessed October 24, 2011), Texas State Historical Association.
71. Donald E. Chipman, "Massanet, Damian," *Handbook of Texas Online*, http://www.tshaonline.org/handbook/online/articles/fma71 (accessed October 24, 2011), Texas State Historical Association.
72. Diana Hadley, Thomas H. Naylor and Mardith K. Schuetz-Miller, *The Presidio and Militia of the Northern Frontier of New Spain: A Documentary History*, vol. 2, part 2, *1700–1765* (Tucson: University of Arizona Press, 1997), 324, n. 20.
73. Vivian Elizabeth Smyrl, "Guadalupe River," *Handbook of Texas Online*, http://www.tshaonline.org/handbook/online/articles/rng01 (accessed August 21, 2011), Texas State Historical Association.
74. David J. Webber, *The Spanish Frontier in North America* (New Haven, CT: Yale University Press, 1994).
75. Dunn, "Apache Relations."
76. "Urrutia, Jose De," *Handbook of Texas Online*, http://www.tshaonline.org/handbook/online/articles/fur03 (accessed August 16, 2011), Texas State Historical Association.

77. Robert S. Weddle, *The San Saba Mission* (College Station: Texas A&M University Press, 1999), 15.
78. Donald E. Chipman, "Urrutia, Toribio De," *Handbook of Texas Online*, http://www.tshaonline.org/handbook/online/articles/fur06 (accessed October 24, 2011), Texas State Historical Association.
79. Maria de Fátima Wade, *The Native Americans of the Texas Edwards Plateau, 1582–1799* (Austin: University of Texas Press, 2003), 176.
80. Nancy McGown Minor, *Turning Adversity to Advantage: A History of the Lipan Apaches of Texas and Northern Mexico, 1700–1900* (New York: University Press, n.d.), 32.
81. Dunn, "Apache Relations," 251.
82. Ibid.
83. *San Pedro Springs*, http://www.edwardsaquifer.net/spspring.html (accessed December 6, 2011).
84. Robert S. Weddle, *San Juan Bautista, Gateway to Spanish Texas* (Austin: University of Texas Press, 1968).
85. *Mapa de Toda la Frontera de los Dominios Del Rey en la America Septentrional.* Original map in the Ministerio del Ejerite Servicio Geografico, Session Topografia, Madrid.
86. Minor, *Turning Adversity to Advantage*, 44.
87. "Pavo Real," *Texas Beyond History*, http://www.texasbeyondhistory.net/pavoreal/site.html (accessed January 15, 2007).
88. Ibid.
89. Minor, *Turning Adversity to Advantage*, 34.
90. The Pedernales is shown as a branch of the Guadalupe on Lafora's map of 1771.
91. Minor, *Turning Adversity to Advantage*, 37.
92. "Los Almagres, the Lost Spanish Mine," *Texas Beyond History*, http://www.texasbeyondhistory.net/plateaus/images/he13.html (accessed December 6, 2011), Texas State Historical Association.
93. Robert S. Weddle, "Los Almagres Mine," *Handbook of Texas Online*, http://www.tshaonline.org/handbook/online/articles/dkl05 (accessed October 2, 2011), Texas State Historical Association.
94. Robert S. Weddle, *The San Saba Mission* (College Station: Texas A&M University Press, 1999), 153.
95. Mariah F. Wade, *Spanish Colonial Documents Pertaining to Mission Santa Cruz de San Sabá (41MN23), Menard County, Texas, with Foreword by Jennifer K. McWilliams and Douglas K. Boyd* (Austin: Archeological Studies Program Report 102, Environmental Affairs Division, Texas Department of

Transportation, and Report of Investigations Number 154, Prewitt and Associates, Inc., Cultural Resources Services, 2007).

96. Jeffrey D. Carlisle, "Apache Indians," *Handbook of Texas Online*, http://www.tshaonline.org/handbook/online/articles/bma33 (accessed November 20, 2011), Texas State Historical Association.

97. *Mapa de Toda la Frontera de los Dominios Del Rey en la America Septentrional.* Original map in the Ministerio del Ejerite Servicio Geografico, Session Topografia, Madrid.

98. Minor, *Turning Adversity to Advantage*, 64.

99. Texas State Historic Marker 5327004212 (N30 55.338, W099 48.160).

100. *Presidio San Luis de las Amarillas*, http://www.menardtexas.com/Presidio/presidio.htm (accessed December 6, 2011).

101. Nicholas De Lafora and Lawrence Kinnaird, *The Frontiers of New Spain Nicolas De Lafora's Description, 1766–1768*, 1st ed. (n.p.: Quivera Society, 1958); Dennis Reinhartz and Gerald D. Saxon, *Mapping an Empire: Soldier-Engineers on the Southwestern Frontier* (n.p.: University of Texas Press, 2005), 67.

102. Ibid.

CHAPTER 4

103. *Lipan Apache Indian History*, http://www.accessgenealogy.com/native/tribes/apache/lipan.htm (accessed February 1, 2007).

104. William Edward Dunn, "Apache Relations in Texas, 1718–1750," *Southwestern Historical Quarterly Online* 14, no. 3 (n.d.): 198–269.

105. T.R. Fehrenbach, *The Destruction of a People* (New York: Alfred A. Knopf, 1974; Reprint, DaCapo Press, 1994), 197.

106. "Pavo Real," *Texas Beyond History*.

107. Minor, *Turning Adversity to Advantage*, 8.

108. Dunn, "Apache Relations."

109. Jean Louis Berlandier, *The Indians of Texas in 1830*, translated by Patricia Reading Leclerq (Washington, D.C.: Smithsonian Institution Press, 1969).

110. T.S. Dennis and Mrs. T.S. Dennis, *The Life of F.M. Buckelew, The Indian Captive as Related by Himself* (Bandera, TX: Hunter's Printing House, 1925).

111. Herman Lehmann, *Nine Years among the Indians, 1870–1879*, edited by J. Marvin Hunter (Austin, TX: Von Beockmann-Jones Company, 1927).

112. J. Marvin Hunter, *The Boy Captives: Being the True Story of the Experiences and Hardships of Clinton L. Smith and Jeff D. Smith* (San Saba, TX: San Saba Printing, 2002).

113. Berlandier, *Indians of Texas.*
114. Jose Francisco Ruiz, *Report on the Indian Tribes of Texas in 1828*, facsimile and translation edited with an introduction by John C. Ewers and translated by Georgette Dorn (New Haven, CT: Yale University Press, 1972).
115. Minor, *Turning Adversity to Advantage.*
116. Minor, *Light Gray People*, 54–55.
117. Dennis, *Life of F.M. Buckelew.*
118. Ibid.
119. Berlandier, *Indians of Texas.*
120. Dennis, *Life of F.M. Buckelew.*
121. Minor, *Light Gray People*, 57–58,
122. Berlandier, *The Indians of Texas in 1830.*
123. Frederick C. Chabot and Carlos Castañeda, trans., *Fray Juan Agustin de Morfi: Memories for the History of the Province of Texas, Indian Excerpts* (San Antonio, TX: Naylor Publishing Company, 1932).
124. Herbert Eugene Bolton, *Texas in the Middle Eighteenth Century* (Berkeley: University of California Press, 1915).
125. Wade, *Native Americans of the Texas Edwards Plateau*, 176.
126. Minor, *Turning Adversity to Advantage*, 109.
127. Kerr WMA, http://www.tpwd.state.tx.us/huntwild/hunt/wma/find_a_wma/list/?id=12 (accessed December 6, 2011).
128. Mike Bowlin, "Boneyard Water Hole Massacre Site," *Kerrville Daily Times*, September 15, 1991.
129. Thomas F. Schilz, "Castro, Cuelgas De," *Handbook of Texas Online*, http://www.tshaonline.org/handbook/online/articles/fca92 (accessed October 25, 2011), Texas State Historical Association.
130. Stephen L. Moore, *Savage Frontier*, vol. 4, *1842–1845* (n.p.: University of North Texas Press, 2010), 217.
131. "Flacco (abt. 1790–abt. 1850)," Lipan Apache Tribe of Texas, http://www.lipanapache.org/Museum/museum_chiefs.html (accessed December 6, 2011).
132. Joseph Luther, "Lipan Apaches in the Texas Hill Country," *Kerrville Daily Times*, September 2010.
133. Thomas A. Britten, *The Lipan Apaches, People of Wind and Lightning* (Albuquerque: University of New Mexico Press, 2009), 230.
134. Ibid., 60–61.
135. Lipan Apache Band of Texas, http://www.lipanapachebandoftexas.com/index.html (accessed December 6, 2011).

CHAPTER 5

136. "Comanche," *Wikipedia*, http://en.wikipedia.org/wiki/Comanche (accessed December 6, 2011).
137. Pekka Hämäläinen, *The Comanche Empire* (New Haven, CT: Yale University Press, 2008).
138. David G. Burnet, "The Comanches and Other Tribes of Texas; and the Policy to be Pursued Respecting Them," in *Historical and Statistical Information Respecting the History, Conditions, and Prospects of the Indian Tribes of the United States*, edited by Henry R. Schoolcraft, 9 vols. (Philadelphia: Lippincott, Grambo, 1851).
139. Betty, *Comanche Society*, 68–69.
140. Carol A. Lipscomb, "Comanche Indians," *Handbook of Texas Online*, http://www.tshaonline.org/handbook/online/articles/bmc72 (accessed August 27, 2011), Texas State Historical Association.
141. T.R. Fehrenbach, *Comanches: The Destruction of a People* (New York: DaCapo Press, 1994).
142. Gwynne, *Empire of the Summer Moon*, 89; Fehrenbach, *Comanches*.
143. Fehrenbach, *Comanches*, 145.
144. Thomas W. Kavanagh, *The Comanches: A History, 1706–1875* (Lincoln: University of Nebraska Press, 1999), 94.
145. This location is shown on a map by Henderson K. Yoakum, New Philippines, Content 1805–1819, map ca. 1855. Map appears as the frontispiece of *History of Texas*, by Henderson Yoakum. This same trail is also shown in John Sayles and Henry Sayles, "Map of Spanish Texas 1835," *Early Laws of Texas, 1731–1876*, vol. 1 (St. Louis, MO: Gilbert Book Company, 1891).
146. Sayles, "Map of Spanish Texas."
147. Ben E. Pingenot, "Fort Clark," *Handbook of Texas Online*, http://www.tshaonline.org/handbook/online/articles/qbf10 (accessed November 13, 2011), Texas State Historical Association.
148. Fehrenbach, *Comanches*, 251.
149. Campbell, *Gone to Texas*, 63.
150. Fehrenbach, *Comanches*, 253, 267.
151. George Catlin, *North American Indians*, edited by Peter Matthiessen (New York: Penguin Books, 1989).
152. Betty, *Comanche Society*, 87.
153. Berlandier, *Indians of Texas.*.

154. La Segunda Compañía Volante de San Carlos de Parras, a company of one hundred Spanish colonial mounted lancers. Their lasting legacy would be to give their name to the former Mission San Antonio de Valero that would become known as the Alamo because of their association with it. Alamo de Parras, http://www.tamu.edu/faculty/ccbn/dewitt/adp/history/hispanic_period/parras.html (accessed December 6, 2011).
155. Berlandier, *Indians of Texas.*
156. Ibid.
157. Ibid.
158. Fehrenbach, *Comanches*, 305.
159. Ibid., 315.
160. Olive Dixon, *Life of Billy Dixon* (Dallas, TX: Southwest Press, 1914).
161. Betty, *Comanche Society*, 87–88.
162. Fehrenbach, *Comanches*, 124.
163. Hunter, *Boy Captives*, 166.
164. Jodye Lynn Dickson Schilz, "Council House Fight," *Handbook of Texas Online*, http://www.tshaonline.org/handbook/online/articles/btc01 (accessed November 13, 2011), Texas State Historical Association; Walter Prescott Webb, *The Texas Rangers* (Boston: Houghton Mifflin, 1935; Reprint, Austin: University of Texas Press, 1982).
165. Rupert N. Richardson, *The Comanche Barrier to South Plains Settlement: A Century and a Half of Savage Resistance to the Advancing White Frontier* (n.p.: Arthur H. Clarke Co., 1933).
166. Carol A. Lipscomb, "Comanche Indians," *Handbook of Texas Online*, http://www.tshaonline.org/handbook/online/articles/bmc72 (accessed November 13, 2011), Texas State Historical Association.
167. Jodye Lynn Dickson Schilz, "Buffalo Hump," *Handbook of Texas Online*, http://www.tshaonline.org/handbook/online/articles/fbu12 (accessed November 13, 2011), Texas State Historical Association.
168. Rudolph L. Biesele, *The History of the German Settlements in Texas, 1831–1861* (Austin, TX: Von Boeckmann-Jones, 1930, 1964).
169. Joseph Luther, "The Penateka Comanche," *Kerrville Daily Times*, July 23, 2010.
170. Lipscomb, "Comanche Indians."
171. Branley Allan Branson and Mary Lou Branson, "Ferment on the Frontier: The Story of the Buffalo Soldiers," *World and I* 13, no. 2 (1998): 186.
172. Clara Watkins, *Kerr County Texas: 1856–1976* (Kerrville, TX: Hill Country Preservation Society, Inc., n.d.), 162–63.

173. *Galveston Daily News,* January 5, 1877, as quoted in Matilda Real, "A History of Kerr County, Texas" (master's thesis, University of Texas, 1942), 54.
174. Texas State Historical Marker 5265005324, (N30 09.273,W099 20.470).
175. *Satanta,* http://www.tsl.state.tx.us/treasures/indians/satanta.html (accessed February 9, 2007).
176. Jerrold E. Levy, "Kiowa," *Handbook of North American Indians* 13, no. 2 (2001): 907–25, Smithsonian Institution, Washington, BIA 1854–1857.
177. Nancy Kenmotsu, "Kiowa," *Texas Beyond History,* http://www.texasbeyondhistory.net/plateaus/peoples/kiowa.html (accessed December 6, 2011).
178. Mildred P. Mayhall, *The Kiowas* (Norman: University of Oklahoma Press, 1962; Reprint, 1971).

CHAPTER 6

179. E. Charles Palmer, "Land Use and Cultural Change along the Balcones Escarpment: 1718–1986," in Patrick L. Abbott and C.M. Woodruff Jr., eds., *The Balcones Escarpment* (Central Texas: Geological Society of America, 1986), 153–62.
180. David J. Weber, *The Mexican Frontier, 1821–1846: The American Southwest under Mexico* (Albuquerque: University of New Mexico Press, 1982), 26.
181. Ruben Rendon Lozano, *Viva Tejanos: The Story of the Tejanos, the Mexican-born Patriots of the Texas Revolution,* with new material added by Mary Ann Noonan Guerra (San Antonio, TX: Alamo Press, ca. 1936; Reprint, 1985).
182. Adán Benavides Jr., "Tejano," *Handbook of Texas Online,* http://www.tshaonline.org/handbook/online/articles/pft07 (accessed August 31, 2011), Texas State Historical Association.
183. Andrés Tijerina, *Tejanos and Texas under the Mexican Flag, 1821–1836* (College Station: Texas A&M University Press, 1994), 22–23.
184. *Bexareños,* http://bexargenealogy.com/page13.html (accessed December 6, 2011).
185. Tijerina, *Tejanos and Texas.*
186. *La Segunda Compañía Volante de San Carlos de Parras,* http://www.tamu.edu/faculty/ccbn/dewitt/parrasco.htm (accessed December 6, 2011).
187. *Alamo de Parras,* http://www.tamu.edu/ccbn/dewitt/adp/ (accessed February 5, 2007).

188. Bernice Strong, "Ruiz, Jose Francisco," *Handbook of Texas Online*, http://www.tshaonline.org/handbook/online/articles/fru11 (accessed October 14, 2011), Texas State Historical Association.
189. Randell G. Tarín, "Second Flying Company of San Carlos De Parras," *Handbook of Texas Online*, http://www.tshaonline.org/handbook/online/articles/qhs01 (accessed October 4, 2011), Texas State Historical Association.
190. Berlandier, *Indians of Texas.*
191. Jose Francisco Ruiz, *Report on the Indian tribes of Texas in 1828*, Western Americana series, no. 5 (New Haven, CT: Yale University Library, 1972).
192. "José Francisco Ruiz," Texas Historical Association, http://www.tamu.edu/faculty/ccbn/dewitt/adp/history/bios/ruiz/ruiz.html (accessed December 6, 2011).
193. Berlandier quoted in Pekka Hämäläinen,, *The Comanche Empire* (New Haven, CT: Yale University Press, 2009), 145.
194. T.R. Fehrenbach, *Lone Star: A History of Texas and the Texans* (New York: DaCapo Press, 2000).

CHAPTER 7

195. Stephen L. Hardin, *Texian Iliad: A Military History of the Texas Revolution* (Austin: University of Texas Press, 1994).
196. Batson, *The Beginning of Kerr County, Texas* (master's thesis, University of Texas–Austin, 1928), 85; Lena Clara Koch, "The Federal Indian Policy in Texas, 1846–1860," *Southwest Historical Quarterly* 29 (n.d.): 24.
197. Rudolph L. Biesele, *The History of the German Settlements in Texas, 1831–1861* (Austin, TX: Von Boeckmann-Jones, 1930; Reprint, 1964).
198. Glen E. Lich, *The German Texans* (San Antonio: University of Texas Institute of Texan Cultures, 1981).
199. C.T. Neu, "Annexation," *Handbook of Texas Online*, http://www.tshaonline.org/handbook/online/articles/mga02 (accessed October 24, 2011), Texas State Historical Association.
200. K. Jack Bauer, "Mexican War," *Handbook of Texas Online*, http://www.tshaonline.org/handbook/online/articles/qdm02 (accessed November 3, 2011), Texas State Historical Association.
201. Campbell, *Gone to Texas*, 189.
202. Dr. Ferdinand Roemer, *Texas; with Particular Reference to German Immigration and the Physical Appearance of the Country*, translated by Oswald Mueller (San Antonio, TX: Standard, 1935; Reprint, German-Texan Heritage Society, 1983; Reprint, Austin, TX: Eakin, 1985).

203. Matt Warnock Turner, *Remarkable Plants of Texas: Uncommon Accounts of Our Common Natives* (Austin: University of Texas Press, 2009), 104.
204. Joseph Luther, "Early Roads of Kerrville: The Old San Antonio Road," *Kerrville Daily Times*, June 30, 2010.
205. Batson, *Kerr County*, 49.
206. Kerr County was named for James Kerr, an "Old Three Hundred" colonist and an important figure in the Texas Revolution.
207. Guido E. Ransleben, *A Hundred Years of Comfort in Texas* (San Antonio, TX: Naylor, 1954; revised ed., 1974).
208. *New York Times*, December 2, 1856.

CHAPTER 8

209. Ben H. Procter, "Texas Rangers," *Handbook of Texas Online*, http://www.tshaonline.org/handbook/online/articles/met04 (accessed November 13, 2011), Texas State Historical Association.
210. Fehrenbach, *Comanches*, 298–99.
211. Ibid.
212. *DeWitt Colony Defense*, www.tamu.edu/ccbn/dewitt/Defense.htm (accessed December 6, 2011).
213. Paul Lee, "John Coffee Hays: Captain Yack," http://www.theoutlaws.com/heroes2.htm (accessed December 6, 2011).
214. James Kimmins Greer, *Texas Ranger: Jack Hays in the Frontier Southwest* (College Station: Texas A&M University Press, 1993), 29–30.
215. J.W. Wilbarger, *Indian Depredations in Texas* (n.p., 1889), 8.
216. Thomas W. Cutrer, "Walker's Creek, Battle of," *Handbook of Texas Online*, http://www.tshaonline.org/handbook/online/articles/btw02 (accessed May 1, 2011), Texas State Historical Association; Joseph Luther, "The Battle of Walker's Creek," *Kerrville Daily Times*, April 2011.
217. Wilbarger, *Indian Depredations*, 78.
218. Cutrer, "Walker's Creek," *Handbook of Texas Online*.
219. Greer, *Texas Ranger*.
220. Robert M. Utley, *Lone Star Justice: The First Century of the Texas Rangers* (New York: Oxford University Press, 2002), 10; Moore, *Savage Frontier*, 139–52.
221. Wilbarger, *Indian Depredations*, 78.
222. Greer, *Texas Ranger*, 48–49; Bob Bennett, *Kerr County, Texas 1856–1956* (San Antonio, TX: Naylor, 1956), 195–99.
223. Moore, *Savage Frontier*.

224. A.J. Sowell, "The Battle of Bandera Pass," *San Antonio Light*, September 27, 1821, reprinted in *Frontier Times* 2, no. 8 (May 1925): 22–23.
225. Clifford R. Caldwell, *A Days Ride from Here*, vol. I, *Mountain Home* (Caldwell, TX, 2009), 2–3.
226. Andrew Jackson Sowell, *Early Settlers and Indian Fighters of Southwest Texas* (Austin, TX: Ben C. Jones, 1900; Reprint, Austin, TX: State House Press, 1986).
227. J.J. Starkey, "Pioneer History," *Kerrville Times*, December 24, 1952, 7.
228. John Caperton, *Jack Hays: The Intrepid Texas Range* (Bandera, TX: Frontier Times, 1927); Kavanagh, *Comanches*, 268; Moore, *Savage Frontier*, 35.
229. Cox, *Texas Rangers*, 208.
230. Greer, *Texas Ranger*, 29–30.
231. Moore, *Savage Frontier*, 97.
232. *Biographies of Great Lipan Chiefs*, Lipan Apache Tribe of Texas, http://www.lipanapache.org/Museum/museum_chiefs.html (accessed December 6, 2011).
233. Glen E. Lich, "Sansom, John William," *Handbook of Texas Online*, http://www.tshaonline.org/handbook/online/articles/fsa28 (accessed April 26, 2011), Texas State Historical Association.
234. John W. Sansom, *Battle of Nueces River in Kinney County, Tex., Aug. 10, 1862* (n.p., 1905).
235. *Sansom Newsletter*, http://www.armory.com/~vern/family/newsletter/sansom.htm (accessed December 6, 2011).
236. Lich, "Sansom, John William."
237. John Crittenden Duval, *The Adventures of Big Foot Wallace, the Texas Ranger and Hunter* (Macon, GA: Burke, 1870); J. Frank Dobie, "Wallace, William Alexander Anderson [Bigfoot]," *Handbook of Texas Online*, http://www.tshaonline.org/handbook/online/articles/fwa36 (accessed April 18, 2011), Texas State Historical Association.
238. Wilbarger, *Indian Depredations*, 124.
239. Seymour V. Connor, "Ford, John Salmon [Rip]," *Handbook of Texas Online*, http://www.tshaonline.org/handbook/online/articles/ffo11 (accessed November 10, 2011), Texas State Historical Association.
240. Campbell, *Gone to Texas*, 204.
241. John S. "Rip" Ford, *Rip Ford's Texas*, edited by Stephen B. Oates (Austin: University of Texas Press, 1963).
242. Stephen B. Oates, "John S. 'Rip' Ford: Prudent Cavalryman, CSA," *Southwestern Historical Quarterly* 64 (1961): 289–314.

243. E.C. DeMontel, "DeMontel, Charles S.," *Handbook of Texas Online*, http://www.tshaonline.org/handbook/online/articles/fde35 (accessed May 12, 2011), Texas State Historical Association.
244. Ibid.

CHAPTER 9

245. David Paul Smith, *Frontier Defense in the Civil War: Texas Rangers and Rebels* (College Station: Texas A&M University Press, n.d.), 4–5.
246. Ibid., 19.
247. Thomas T. Smith, *The Old Army in Texas: A Research Guide to the U.S. Army in Nineteenth-Century Texas* (Austin: Texas State Historical Association, n.d.).
248. Fehrenbach, *Comanches*, 411.
249. Joseph Luther, "US Army 2nd Dragoon Regiment in Kerr County," *Kerrville Daily Times*, September 2010.
250. Returns from Regular Army Cavalry Regiments, 1833–1916, microfilm no. M744, rolls 14–16.
251. Otis E. Young, *The West of Philip St. George Cooke, 1809–1895* (Glendale, CA: Arthur H. Clark Company, 1955).
252. Thomas T. Smith, "U.S. Army Combat Operations in the Indian Wars of Texas, 1849–1881," *Southwestern Historical Quarterly* 99, no. 4 (1996): 501–31.
253. Philip St. George Cooke, *Scenes and Adventures in the Army or Romances of Military Life* (Philadelphia, 1857).
254. Julius E. DeVos, "Fort Mason," *Handbook of Texas Online*, http://www.tshaonline.org/handbook/online/articles/qbf34 (accessed November 20, 2011), Texas State Historical Association.
255. *Fort McKavett State Historic Site*, Texas Parks and Wildlife Department, http://www.tpwd.state.tx.us/publications/pwdpubs/media/pwd_lf_p4507_0092q.pdf (accessed August 24, 2010).
256. *Second Cavalry Association Regimental History Center*, http://history.dragoons.org (accessed August 25, 2010).
257. Returns from Regular Army Infantry Regiments, June 1821–December 1916, microfilm no. M665, rolls 90–92; Colonel M.L. Crimmins, "Eighth U.S. Infantry in Texas before Civil War," *Frontier Times*, January 4, 1933, 175; Robert Wooster, "Eighth United States Infantry Regiment," *Handbook of Texas Online*, http://www.tshaonline.org/handbook/online/articles/qzemw (accessed November 10, 2011), Texas State Historical Association.
258. R.L. DiNardo and Albert A. Nofi, *James Longstreet: The Man, the Soldier, the Controversy* (n.p.: Combined Books, 19980, 58–59.

259. Irene Van Winkle, "Early Tejano, Polly Rodriguez, Shaped History in Texas," *West Kerr Current*, November 22, 2007, http://wkcurrent.com/early-tejano-polly-rodriguez-shaped-history-in-texas-p1327-71.htm.
260. Bennett, *Kerr County*, 211–16.
261. Jose Policarpo Rodriguez, *Jose Policarpo Rodriguez, "The Old Guide": Surveyor, Scout, Hunter, Indian Fighter, Ranchman, Preacher: His Life in His Own Words* (Nashville, TN: Pub. House of the Methodist Episcopal Church, South, 1897; Reprint, General Books LLC, 2010).
262. Ibid.
263. Charles G. Downing, "Rodriguez, Jose Policarpo," *Handbook of Texas Online*, http://www.tshaonline.org/handbook/online/articles/fro52 (accessed April 20, 2011), Texas State Historical Association.
264. Rudi R. Rodriquez, ed., *A Tejano Son of Texas. An Autobiography by Jose Policarpo "Polly"Rodriguez* (Texas Tejano.com, 2003).

CHAPTER 10

265. Governor E.M. Pease to General T.F. Smith, June 21, 1855, *Military Papers, 1855–1890*, Archives, Texas State Library.
266. *Historical Register and Dictionary of the United States Army*, 493.
267. San Antonio Citadel Club, http://www.citadelsanantonio.org/mexWar.html (accessed December 6, 2011).
268. Cox, *Texas Rangers*, 2008.
269. August Santleben, *A Texas Pioneer: Early Staging and Overland Freighting Days on the Frontiers of Texas and Mexico* (n.p.: The Neale Publishing Company, 1910), 255.
270. Ronnie C. Tyler, "The Callahan Expedition of 1855: Indians or Negroes?" *Southwestern Historical Quarterly* 70 (1967).
271. Manuel Guerra, "Henry, William R.," *Handbook of Texas Online*, http://www.tshaonline.org/handbook/online/articles/fhehg (accessed April 11, 2011), Texas State Historical Association.
272. Ronnie C. Tyler, "Fugitive Slaves in Mexico," *Journal of Negro History* 57, no. 1 (1972).
273. Ford, *Rip Ford's Texas.*
274. Ernest C. Shearer, "The Callahan Expedition, 1855," *Southwestern Historical Quarterly* 54 (October 1951).
275. J.H. Callahan, "Captain Callahan's Address to the People of Texas," *New York Times*, October 26, 1855.

CHAPTER 11

276. George F. Price, *Across the Continent with the Fifth Cavalry* (New York: Van Nostrand, 1883).
277. James R. Arnold, *Jeff Davis's Own: Cavalry, Comanches, and the Battle for the Texas Frontier* (New York: Wiley, 2000).
278. Ibid., 32–36.
279. Price, *Across the Continent*, 31.
280. Arnold, *Jeff Davis's Own*, 32–36.
281. *Little Ice Age*, http://en.wikipedia.org/wiki/Little_Ice_Age (accessed December 6, 2011).
282. Price, *Across the Continent*, 35.
283. United States Army, *Returns from Regular Army Cavalry Regiments*, microfilm no. M744. *Second Cavalry, 1849–1855*, roll 16.
284. Fehrenbach, *Comanches*, 424–25.
285. Sowell, *Early Settlers and Indian Fighters*, 639; United States Army, *Returns from United States Military Posts 1800-1916*, microfilm no. M617, *Camp Verde Tex.: July 1856–Mar. 1869*, roll 1327.
286. Jerry Thompson, *Civil War to the Bloody End: The Life and Times of Major General Samuel P. Heintzelman* (College Station: Texas A&M University Press, 2006).
287. National Archives and Records Administration (NARA), Washington, D.C.; Returns from U.S. Military Posts, 1800–1916; Microfilm Serial, M617, microfilm roll 1327.
288. Ibid.
289. Chris Emmett, *Texas Camel Tales*, Great Texas Books, http://greattexasbooks.org/book/45 (accessed December 6, 2011).
290. Loyd M. Uglow, *Standing in the Gap: Army Outposts, Picket Stations, and the Pacification of the Texas Frontier, 1866–1886* (Forth Worth: Texas Christian University Press, 2001); Roy Eugene Graham, "Federal Fort Architecture in Texas during the Nineteenth Century," *Southwestern Historical Quarterly* 74 (n.d.): 165–88.
291. John Marvin Hunter, *Pioneer History of Bandera County: Seventy-Five Years of Intrepid History* (n.p.: Hunter's Printing House, 1922).
292. Uglow, *Standing in the Gap*, 16.
293. R.E. Lee Jr., *Recollections and Letters of General Robert E. Lee* (New York: Doubleday, 1904).
294. "Indian Massacre," *San Antonio Herald*, March 1856.
295. Price, *Across the Continent*, 57.
296. Ibid.

297. General Orders No. 22, Headquarters of the Army, November 10, 1858.
298. Sowell, *Early Settlers and Indian Fighters*, 646–48.
299. Price, *Across the Continent*, 64.
300. General Orders No. 5, Headquarters Department of Texas, February 13, 1858.
301. Price, *Across the Continent*, 641.
302. Sowell, *Early Settlers and Indian Fighters*, 648.
303. Heintzelman, *Fifty Miles and a Fight*, 83.
304. Ibid., 85.
305. Randolph B. Campbell, "Knights of the Golden Circle," *Handbook of Texas Online*, http://www.tshaonline.org/handbook/online/articles/vbk01 (accessed November 3, 2011), Texas State Historical Association.
306. Jerry Thompson, *Fifty Miles and a Fight: Major Samuel Peter Heintzelman's Journal of Texas and the Cortina War* (Texas State Historical Association, 1998).
307. Price, *Across the Continent*, 84.
308. General Order No. 11, Headquarters of the Army, November 23, 1860.
309. Rebecca J. Herring, "Camp Ives," *Handbook of Texas Online*, http://www.tshaonline.org/handbook/online/articles/qcc21 (accessed April 15, 2011), Texas State Historical Association; United States Army, *Returns from United States Military Posts, 1800–1916*, microfilm no. M617. *Camp Ives Texas: Oct. 1859–Dec. 1860*, roll 1516.
310. John Bell Hood, *Advance and Retreat: Personal Experiences in the United States and Confederate States Armies* (New Orleans, LA: Beauregard, 1880).

Chapter 12

311. National Park Service, *Survey of Historic Sites and Buildings: Camp Verde, Texas*, http://www.nps.gov/history/history/online_books/soldier/sitec16.htm (accessed January 23, 2011).
312. Chris Emmett, *Texas Camel Tales: Incidents Growing Up around an Attempt by the War Department of the United States to Foster an Uninterrupted Flow of Commerce through Texas by the Use of Camels* (n.p.: Naylor, 1933).
313. Odie B. Faulk, *The U.S. Camel Corps: An Army Experiment* (New York: Oxford University Press, 1976).
314. Harlan D. Fowler, *Camels to California* (Stanford, CA: Stanford University Press, 1950), 38.
315. Steve Frangos, "Philip Tedro: A Greek Legend of the American West," *Greek-American Review*, http://www.helleniccomserve.com/philiptedro.htm (accessed January 26, 2011); Fowler, *Camels to California*, 35.

316. Robert Froman, "The Red Ghost," *American Heritage* 11 (April 1961): 35–37, 94–98.
317. Fowler, *Camels to California*, 88.
318. Williams, *Border Ruffians*.
319. Thomas W. Cutrer, "Stanley, David Sloane," *Handbook of Texas Online*, http://www.tshaonline.org/handbook/online/articles/fst12 (accessed April 17, 2011), Texas State Historical Association.
320. Ruth Thomas, *The United States Camel Project in Texas* (master's thesis, Southwest State Teachers College, San Marcos, Texas, 1940), includes photograph of Camels' Leap.
321. Ibid.

CHAPTER 13

322. Jerry Thompson, ed., *Texas and New Mexico on the Eve of the Civil War: The Mansfield and Johnston Inspections, 1859–1861* (n.p.: University of New Mexico Press, 2001), 182.
323. Randolph B. Campbell, "Knights of the Golden Circle," *Handbook of Texas Online*, http://www.tshaonline.org/handbook/online/articles/vbk01 (accessed October 1, 2011), Texas State Historical Association.
324. Price, *Across the Continent*, 95.
325. Robert Underwood Johnson and Clarence Clough Buel, eds., *Battles and Leaders of the Civil War*, vol. 1 (n.p.: Nabu Press; Reprint, 2011).
326. U.S. Secretary of War, Special Order No. 22, January 28, 1861.
327. Thomas Wilhelm, *History of the Eighth U.S. Infantry from Its Organization, in 1838* (Printed at Headquarters, Eighth Infantry, 1873).
328. Thompson, *Texas and New Mexico*, 182.
329. R.H. Williams, *With the Border Ruffians: Memories of the Far West, 1852–1868* (Lincoln, NE: Bison Press, 1982).
330. Bobby D. Weaver, *Castro's Colony: Empresario Development in Texas, 1842–* 1865 (College Station: Texas A&M University Press, 2006), 133; Sowell, *Early Settlers and Indian Fighters*, 164.
331. Francis B. Heitman, *Historical Register*, 993; United States War Department, *War of the Rebellion: A Compilation of the Official Records of the Union and Confederate Armies*, series 1, vol. 1 (Washington, D.C.: Government Printing Office, 1899; hereafter cited as *OR*), 521, 533–34, 552–53, 585; ser. 2, vol. 1, 76.
332. Lonnie R. Speer, *Portals to Hell: Military Prisons of the Civil War* (n.p.: University of Nebraska Press, 2005).

333. Major J.T. Sprague, USA, "Texas, the Secession of Texas, and the Arrest of the United States Officers and Soldiers Serving in Texas," read before the New-York Historical Society, June 25, 1861 (1862); *OR*.
334. *OR*, 122.

CHAPTER 14

335. Thomas W. Cutrer, "Woods, Peter Cavanaugh," *Handbook of Texas Online*, http://www.tshaonline.org/handbook/online/articles/fwo16 (accessed July 31, 2011), Texas State Historical Association.
336. Bradley Folsom, "Third Texas Infantry," *Handbook of Texas Online*, http://www.tshaonline.org/handbook/online/articles/qkt16 (accessed November 3, 2011), Texas State Historical Association.
337. Joe Baluch, "The Dogs of War Unleashed: The Devil Concealed in Men Unchained," *West Texas Historical Association*, 126–41, http://digital.library.schreiner.edu/sldl/pdfs/Baulch.pdf (accessed August 13, 2009).
338. Sylvia Villarreal Bisnar, *P.L. Buquor, Indian Fighter, Texas Ranger, Mayor of San Antonio* (Bloomington, IN: AuthorHouse, 2009), 117–25.
339. Ibid.
340. Ibid.
341. Ibid.
342. Brett J. Derbes, "Second Texas Cavalry," *Handbook of Texas Online*, http://www.tshaonline.org/handbook/online/articles/qks08 (accessed October 2, 2011), Texas State Historical Association.
343. Joseph P. Blessington, *Campaigns of Walker's Texas Division* (New York: Lange, Little, 1875; Reprint, Austin, TX: State House Press, 1994).
344. Brett J. Derbes, "Thirty-sixth Texas Cavalry," *Handbook of Texas Online*, http://www.tshaonline.org/handbook/online/articles/qkt25 (accessed July 31, 2011), Texas State Historical Association.
345. Baluch, "Dogs of War Unleashed."
346. *San Antonio Daily Express*, "Duff, the Rebel Butcher of Western Texas," August 3, 1869.
347. Ibid.
348. Clifford R. Caldwell, *A Day's Ride from Here: Noxville* (Charleston, SC: The History Press, 2011), 30.
349. William Banta and J.W. Coldwell, *Twenty-seven Years on the Texas Frontier* (1893; Reprint, L.G. Park, 1933).
350. G. Ransleben, *A Hundred Years of Comfort in Texas* (San Antonio, TX: Naylor, 1954).

351. Joseph Luther, "Captain Duff's Campaign of Terror–Counter-Insurgency Warfare in the Hill Country," *Kerrville Daily Times*, February 4, 2011.
352. Rodman L. Underwood, *Death on the Nueces: German Texans, Treue der Union* (Austin, TX: Eakin Press, 20000.
353. H.J. Schwethelm, "I Was a Survivor of the Nueces Battle" (as told to Albert Schutze), *San Antonio Press, Frontier Times* section, August 31, 1924; R.H. Williams and John W. Sansom, *Massacre on the Nueces River; Story of a Civil War Tragedy* (Book, n.d.); digital images, http://texashistory.unt.edu/ark:/67531/metapth2409 (accessed December 31, 2010).
354. Treue Der Union (Loyalty to the Union), Texas State History Marker No. 15; National Register Listing No. 78002966.
355. Underwood, *Death on the Nueces*.
356. Bob Bennett, *Kerr County, Texas, 1856–1956* (San Antonio, TX: The Naylor Company, 1956).
357. Most of the narrative is taken from J. Marvin Hunter, "A Bandera County Tragedy," *Frontier Times*, August 1924, 8–11.

CHAPTER 15

358. Texas State Historical Texas 5265000682, Camp Verde, Texas.
359. Stephan Schwartz, *Twenty-two Months a Prisoner of War: A Narrative of Twenty-two Months' Imprisonment by the Confederates, In Texas, through General Twigg's Treachery, Dating from April 1861 to February 1863* (n.p.: A.F. Nelson, 1891; Reprint, General Books, 2010).
360. Jerry Thompson, *Texas and New Mexico*, 183.
361. Schwartz, *Twenty-two Months*, 21.
362. Ibid.
363. *OR*, ser. 2, vol. 1, part 1.
364. *Kerrville Mountain Sun*, March 22, 1984.
365. Schwartz, *Twenty-two Months*, 32.
366. Ibid.
367. Ibid., 32–33.
368. Ibid., 37.

CHAPTER 16

369. David Paul Smith, *Frontier Defense in the Civil War: Texas' Rangers and Rebels* (College Station: Texas A&M University Press, 1992).

370. Texas State Historical Marker 3823, Bandera.

371. Mike Cox, *The Texas Rangers*, vol. 1, *Wearing the Cinco Peso, 1821–1900* (New York: Tom Doherty Associates, 2008), 175.

372. Kerr County Historical Commission, *Kerr County Album* (n.p.: Taylor Publishing Company, 1986), 54–55.

373. David Paul Smith, "McCord, James Ebenezer," *Handbook of Texas Online*, http://www.tshaonline.org/handbook/online/articles/fmc20 (accessed October 2, 2011), Texas State Historical Association.

374. Caldwell, *A Day's Ride*, 47.

375. Darren L. Ivey, *Texas Rangers: A Registry and History* (n.p.: McFarland, 2010).

376. Jayhawker is defined as a Unionist guerrilla.

377. Robert Dunnam, "Frontier Regiment," *Handbook of Texas Online*, http://www.tshaonline.org/handbook/online/articles/qjf01 (accessed April 16, 2011), Texas State Historical Association.

378. Ibid.

379. *OR*, ch. 46, vol. 8, *Correspondence, Etc.-Confederate*, 819.

Chapter 17

380. Louis J. Wortham, *History of Texas from Wilderness to Commonwealth* (n.p.: Wortham-Molyneaux Co., 1924).

381. Forrest Carter, *The Rebel Outlaw: Josey Wales* (n.p.: Whippoorwill Publishers, 1972; republished in 1975 as *Gone to Texas*).

382. Charles W. Ramsdell, "Texas from the Fall of the Confederacy to the Beginning of Reconstruction," *Quarterly of the Texas State Historical Association* 11 (January 1908).

383. Fehrenbach, *Comanches*, 494.

384. Bruce A. Glasrud and Michael N. Searles, eds., *Buffalo Soldiers in the West: A Black Soldiers Anthology* (College Station: Texas A&M University Press, 2007).

385. Branson, "Ferment on the Frontier," 186.

386. Rebecca Bush, *The Kickapoo Traditional Tribe of Texas*, http://www.texasindians.com/kickapoo.htm (accessed March 3, 2011).

387. Arrell M. Gibson, *The Kickapoos, Lords of the Middle Border* (Norman: University of Oklahoma Press, 1963).

388. Felipe A. Latorre and Dolores L. Latorre, *The Mexican Kickapoo Indians* (Austin: University of Texas Press, 1976).

389. Joseph Luther, "The Kickapoo Campaigns, Camp Verde After in the War," *Kerrville Daily Times*, March 2011.

390. Kickapoo Lucky Eagle Casino, http://www.luckyeagletexas.com (accessed March 3, 2011).
391. Ramsdell, "Texas from the Fall of the Confederacy."
392. M.L. Crimmins, "The Fourth Cavalry in Texas," *Frontier Times Magazine* 15, no. 5 (February 1938).
393. A sutler's store is an establishment on an army post intended to sell provisions to the soldiers.
394. Heintzelman, *Fifty Miles and a Fight*, 329.
395. Crimmins, "Fourth Cavalry in Texas."
396. United States National Archives, *U.S. Returns from Military Posts, 1806–1916*, Microfilm 1327, Camp Verde, January 1868.
397. George W. Cullum, *Biographical Register of the Graduates of the Military Academy*, vol. 2 (n.p.: Nabu Press, 1911).
398. *Summary of Reports of 5th Military District, 1866–1870*, http://en.wikipedia.org/wiki/Fifth_Military_District (accessed December 6, 2011).
399. Santleben, *Texas Pioneer*, 267.
400. Emmett, *Texas Camel Tales*.
401. William L. Richter, *The Army in Texas during Reconstruction, 1865–1870* (College Station: Texas A&M University Press, 1987).
402. Sowell, *Early Settlers and Indian Fighters*, 552.
403. Crimmins, "The Fourth Cavalry in Texas."
404. Charles W. Ramsdell, *Reconstruction in Texas* (New York: Columbia University Press, 1910; Reprint, Austin: Texas State Historical Association, 1970).
405. Cecil Harper Jr., "Freedmen's Bureau," *Handbook of Texas Online*, http://www.tshaonline.org/handbook/online/articles/ncf01 (accessed November 3, 2011), Texas State Historical Association.
406. Claude Elliott, "The Freedmen's Bureau in Texas," *Southwestern Historical Quarterly* 56 (July 1952); William Lee Richter, *Overreached on All Sides: The Freedmen's Bureau Administrators in Texas, 1865–1868* (College Station: Texas A&M University Press, 1991).
407. Carl H. Moneyhon, *Texas after the Civil War: The Struggle of Reconstruction* (College Station: Texas A&M University Press, n.d.)
408. Santleben, *Texas Pioneer*, 268.

Chapter 18

409. Texas Military Forces Historical Sketch, "1870 to 1879" http://www.texasmilitaryforcesmuseum.org/tnghist13.htm (accessed December 12, 2011).
410. Adjutant General's Department, Texas Volunteer Guard military rolls, *Texas State Militia*, Texas State Library and Archives Commission.
411. Christina Stopka, *Partial List of Texas Ranger Company and Unit Commanders*, Texas Ranger Research Center, n.d., http://www.texasranger.org/ReCenter/captains.pdf (accessed December 6, 2011). Henry Schwethelm, a survivor of the Unionist group massacred at the Nueces River, Texas, in August 1862, left an account of events in 1923 that originally appeared in the *San Antonio Express* newspaper in August 1924 and also in the *Bandera Frontier Times* 2, no. 1 (October 1924).
412. Joseph Luther, "Shootout at Schreiner's: 1873 Gunfight in Downtown Kerrville," *Kerrville Daily Times*, June 21, 2010.
413. Texas State Historical Marker #4831. Catherine "Kate" Ringer McLaurin (sometimes McLauren) was with her three small children and fourteen-year-old Allen Lease in the garden when a band of Lipan Apaches started to plunder her home. Lease, thinking there were pigs in the house, went to investigate the noise and was shot and killed. Catherine was also shot, dying hours later, but her children were unharmed. Maud, age six, went for help because her father, John McLaurin, was away. Neighbors gave chase for seventy miles before soldiers from Fort Clark took command. Soldiers trailed the party into Mexico, reportedly killing all but two.
414. Kerr County Historical Commission, *Kerr County Album*, 122–23.

Chapter 19

415. "Frontier Battalion," *Handbook of Texas Online*, http://www.tshaonline.org/handbook/online/articles/qqf01 (accessed July 11, 2011), Texas State Historical Association.
416. Darren L. Ivey, *The Texas Rangers: A Registry and History* (n.p.: McFarland, 2010), 143.
417. Cox, *Texas Rangers*, 193.
418. *Texas Almanac for 1871*.
419. *Frontier Times*, "Neal Caldwell, A Gallant Texas Ranger," January 1926, 8–15.
420. James B. Gillette, *Six Years with the Texas Rangers, 1875 to 1881* (New Haven, CT: Yale University Press, n.d.), 63.

CONCLUSION

421. *Kerrville Times*, July 30, 1931.
422. *Kerrville Daily Times*, June 1, 1956.
423. Bennett, *Kerr County.*
424. John Williams died in Kerr County in 1860; he appears in the 1860 census.
425. Bennett, *Kerr County,* 55.
426. Rebecca J. Herring, "Camp Verde, TX," *Handbook of Texas Online*, http://www.tshaonline.org/handbook/online/articles/hrc16 (accessed April 20, 2011), Texas State Historical Association.
427. Camp Verde General Store, http://campverdegeneralstore.com/main/index.php.
428. Hazard, *Frontier in American Literature.*
429. Roundtree, *Notes on the Last of the Mohicans.*
430. Turner, *Rise of the New West.*
431. Michael Blake, *Dances with Wolves* (n.p.: Hrymfaxe LLC, 2002).

Selected Bibliography

Arnold, James R. *Jeff Davis's Own: Cavalry, Comanches, and the Battle for the Texas Frontier*. New York: Wiley, 2000.

Berlandier, Jean Louis. *The Indians of Texas in 1830*. Translated by Patricia Reading Leclerq. Washington, D.C.: Smithsonian Institution Press, 1969.

Britten, Thomas A. *The Lipan Apaches, People of Wind and Lightning*. Albuquerque: University of New Mexico Press, 2009.

Caldwell, Clifford R. *A Day's Ride from Here: Noxville, Texas*. Charleston, SC: The History Press, 2011.

Chipman, Donald E. *Spanish Texas, 1519–1821*. Austin: University of Texas Press, 1992.

Cox, Mike. *The Texas Rangers*. Vol. I, *Wearing the Cinco Peso 1821–1900*. New York: Tom Doherty Associates, 2008.

De Lafora, Nicholas, and Lawrence Kinnaird. *The Frontiers of New Spain Nicholas De Lafora's Description, 1766–1768*. Berkeley, CA: Quivira Society, 1958.

Emmett, Chris. *Texas Camel Tales; Incidents Growing Up Around an Attempt by the War Department of the United States to Foster an Uninterrupted Flow of Commerce Through Texas by the Use of Camels*. San Antonio, TX: Naylor, 1932.

Fehrenbach, T.R. *Comanches: The Destruction of a People*. New York: Alfred A. Knopf, 1974. Reprint, DaCapo Press, 1994.

———. *Lone Star: A History of Texas and the Texans*. New York: De Capo Press, 2000.

Greer, James K. *Texas Ranger: Jack Hays in the Frontier Southwest*. College Station: Texas A&M University Press, 1993.

Gwynne, S.C. *Empire of the Summer Moon: Quanah Parker and the Rise and Fall of the Comanches, the Most Powerful Indian Tribe in American History*. New York: Scribner, 2010.

Hester, Thomas R. "Early Human Populations along the Balcones Escarpment." In *The Balcones Escarpment, Central Texas*. Edited by Patrick L. Abbott and C.M. Woodruff Jr. Geological Society of America, 1986. Reprint, Center for Archeological Research, the University of Texas at San Antonio, http://www.lib.utexas.edu/geo/balcones_escarpment/pages55-62.html.

Minor, Nancy McGowen. *The Light Gray People: An Ethno-History of the Lipan Apaches of Texas and Northern Mexico*. Lanham, MD: University Press of America, 2009.

———. *Turning Adversity to Advantage: A History of the Lipan Apaches of Texas and Northern Mexico, 1700–1900*. Lanham, MD: University Press of America, 2009.

Moore, Stephen L. *Savage Frontier*. Vol. 4, *1842–1845: Rangers, Riflemen and Indian Wars in Texas*. Denton: University of North Texas Press, 2010.

Newcomb, W.W., Jr. *The Indians of Texas: From Prehistoric to Modern Times*. Austin: University of Texas Press, 1961.

Price, George F. *Across the Continent with the Fifth Cavalry*. New York: Van Nostrand, 1883.

Ransleben, Guido E. *A Hundred Years of Comfort in Texas*. San Antonio, TX: Naylor, 1954.

Schwartz, Stephen. *Twenty-two Months a Prisoner of War*. St. Louis, MO: A.F. Nelson Publishing Co., 1891.

Simpson, Harold B. *Cry Comanche: The Second U.S. Cavalry in Texas*. Hillsboro, TX: Hill Junior College Press, 1979.

Smith, David Paul. *Frontier Defense in the Civil War: Texas Rangers and Rebels*. College Station: Texas A&M Press, 1992.

Turner, Ellen Sue, Thomas R. Hester and Richard L. McReynolds. *A Field Guide to Stone Artifacts of Texas Indians*. Lanham, MD: Taylor Trade Publishing, 2011.

Underwood, Rodman L. *Death on the Nueces: German Texans, Treue der Union*. Austin, TX: Eakin Press, 2000.

Wade, Mariah, and Don R. Wade. *The Native Americans of the Edwards Plateau*. Austin: University of Texas Press, 2003.

Weddle, Robert S. *The San Saba Mission: Spanish Pivot in Texas*. College Station: Texas A&M University Press. 1999.

Williams, R.H. *With the Border Ruffians: Memories of the Far West, 1852–1868*. Lincoln, NE: Bison Press, 1982.

Index

A

Adelsverein 66
Alamo de Parras 52, 62
Alarcón, Martín de 29
Alexander, Major W.J. 124, 131
Ames Model 1840 cavalry saber 87
annexation 67
Apache 106
Apache rancherias 40
Apachería 39
Apache Trail 153
Archaic Period 19
Arroyo de la Soledad 13
atlatl 19
Austin, Stephen F. 71

B

Balcones Escarpment 12, 18, 19, 39, 49, 52, 56, 66
Balcones Fault Zone 12
bald cypress 69
Bandera Home Guards 88
Bandera Pass 14, 52, 73, 76, 83, 91, 92, 98, 135
Bandera Pass Cemetery 91
Battle of Bandera Pass 75
Battle of Devils River 106
Battle of Dove Creek 136
Battle of the Alamo 65
Battle of the Nueces 77, 122
Battle of Walker's Creek 73
Beale, Lieutenant Edward Fitzgerald 109
Bee, General Hamilton 120
Benton, Captain Nathaniel 92
Berlandier, Jean Louis 40, 42, 52, 63
Béxar County 65
Béxar District 61
Bexareños 62
Béxar Provincial Militia 62
Bidais 22
Blue Duck 58
Boneyard 44, 45, 103
Bonnell, Captain John A. 149

Bonnell, Will H. 149
bow and arrow 19, 20, 24, 42, 54
Bowie, Jim 35
Bowman, C.S. 138
Brackett, Albert G. 115
Brown, Joshua D. 69
Buckelew, Frank M. 40, 42
Buffalo Hump 55, 56, 57, 79
Buquor, Captain Pasquale Leo 118
Burbank, Major Sidney 115
burned rock middens 17, 20
Burney, H.M. 123

C

Caddos 23
Caldwell, James N. 115
Callahan, Captain James Hughes 90
Callan, Captain James J. 131
Camel Experiment 107
Camels' Leap 111
Camino de Tehuacanas 33
Camino Pinta 33
Camp Béxar 82
Camp Cooper 96, 104
Camp Davant 83, 90
Camp Davis 118, 121, 131
Camp Houston 82
Camp Ives 83, 104, 105, 114, 135
Camp Pedernales 122
Camp Verde 13, 22, 33, 38, 39, 40, 48, 60, 63, 66, 67, 72, 75, 77, 83, 87, 88, 90, 94, 98, 100, 104, 107, 114, 115, 116, 117, 118, 120, 124, 127, 132, 135, 137, 147, 149, 159, 172
Camp Verde, CSA 130
Camp Verde Historic Park 152
Camp Verde Ranch 149
Camp Verde Store 49, 102, 150
Camp Verde, USA, is closed 140
Camp Wood 83
cannibalism 26, 43
Cañon de Ugalde 13, 73
Castro, Cuelgas de 45
Catlin, George 51
Cedar Ridge 27
Center Point 46, 69
Center Point Cemetery 150
Cerro del Almagre 35
Chambliss, William 98
Chief Flacco 45
Ciudadanos Armados 62
Clear Fork of the Brazos River 57
Clovis culture 17
Coahuila y Tejas 60
Coahuiltecan 21, 24
Coahuiltecos 24
Coahuiltejano 61
Coldwell, Captain Neil 148
Collins, Corporal Patrick 105
Colorados, Cabellos 43
Colt .36-caliber navy revolvers 95
Colt Dragoon handgun 86
Comanche 47, 49, 52, 57, 63, 65, 71, 73, 75, 78, 83, 96, 102, 104, 105, 135, 137
Comanche barrier 49
Comancheria 48
Comanche Trail 49, 50
Comfort 69, 123
Constitución Federal de los Estados Unidos Mexicanos de 1824 61
Cooke, Lieutenant Colonel St. George 84
Cortina War 105

Council House Fight 55
Cuero de Coyote 31, 44
Curry's Creek 69

D

Davis, Captain Henry T. 121
Davis, Jefferson 94
Davis's Company of Texas State Troops 117
DeMontel, Captain Charles S. 72, 80, 131
Department of Béxar 65
Department of Texas 81
Domingo Terán de los Rios 30
Donnelson, Captain John 117
Dowdy children 57
Duff, Captain James 120
Duff's Company of Texas Partisan Rangers 117

E

Early Archaic 19
Edwards Plateau 11, 48, 52, 82
Eighth U.S. Infantry 83, 127
Eighth U.S. Infantry Band 127
Eighth U.S. Infantry Regiment 87
El Campo Verde 16, 27, 30
El Indio 137
El Nacimiento 136
encomienda 27
Estados Unidos de Mexicanos 60
Euro-American colonists 60
Euro-American colonization 71

F

Fifth U.S. Infantry 140
First Federal Line 82
First Texas Cavalry, USA 77
First Texas Mounted Rifles 80
First U.S. Artillery 98, 104
First U.S. Infantry 82, 83, 98, 104, 116, 126
Flacco 45, 72, 76
Flores, Bernardo de Miranda y 35
Ford, Captain John S. (Rip) 72, 79, 92, 119
Fort Belknap 96, 104
Fort Brown 104
Fort Clark 83
Fort Croghan 82, 84
Fort Davis 88
Fort Duncan 82, 93, 104
Fort Inge 82, 84
Fort Lincoln 82, 84, 87
Fort Lugubre 86
Fort Martin Scott 82, 84, 137
Fort Mason 83, 84, 96, 137
Fort McIntosh 104
Fort McKavett 83, 86
Fort Sam Houston 82
Fort Terrett 83, 86
Fourteenth Reserve Militia 143
Fourteenth Texas Cavalry Battalion 122
Fourth U.S. Cavalry 137
Franciscans 24, 34
Fray Damián Massanet 30
Fredericksburg 56, 67
Freedmen's Bureau 141
Frio River 50
Frio Trail 50, 102, 105

Frontier Battalion 146
Frontier Forces 147
Frontier Organization 132
Frontier Regiment 80, 130

G

Ganahl, Dr. Charles A. 115
Gatlin site 19
Goss, Spence 103
Graham, Lieutenant W.M. 98, 127
Great Western Trail 154
Green Lake 113
Guadalupe River 12, 30, 31, 33, 38, 44, 48, 49, 63, 65, 66, 69, 74, 98, 122

H

hangerbande 117
Harbour, H.T. 123
Hardee, Lieutenant Colonel William J. 86
Hasinais 22
Hatch, John P. 138
Hays, Captain John Coffee 45, 68, 72, 73, 76
headwaters of the Guadalupe River 22, 84
Heintzelman, Major Samuel P. 104, 137
Henry, Captain William R. 91
Hi Jolly 108, 109
Historical Marker 682 101
Historical Marker 4748 101
Historic Period 22
Holmes, Captain Stokely M. 117, 128
Holmes, Major Stokely M. 120
Hood, Lieutenant John Bell 83, 94, 106
Hunter, Major James M. 121

I

Ingenhuett, Thomas 123

J

Jeff Davis's Own 94
Johnston, Albert Sidney 94
Jumano 25
Juneteenth 137, 141

K

Kerr County 11, 57, 65, 69, 76, 83, 102, 105, 112, 135, 143
Kerr County Minutemen 123, 144
Kerr County's Company I, Texas Militia 143
Kerrville 63, 69, 83, 103, 104, 140
Kerrville Mountaineers 145
Kerrville Mounted Rifles 145
Kickapoo 45, 135, 136, 138, 139, 140
King, Captain J.H. 98
Kiowa 58, 106, 135
Kiowa chief Santanta 58
Knights of the Golden Circle 105, 113

L

Labor de los Lipanes 63
Lafora, Nicolás de 36
Lafora's 1771 map 33, 35, 37
Lane, E.C. 102
La Puerta de Las Casas Viejas 29, 33

La Rivera 31, 44
Las Moras Springs 50
last battle of Bandera Pass 140
last Indian raids in Kerr County 57
last Lipan Apache raid in Kerr County 46
last permanent Indian campground in Kerr County 45
last raid by Lipan Apaches in Frio Canyon 144
last soldiers assigned to Camp Verde 140
Late Prehistoric Period 20
Lawhorn, Captain John 124, 131
Lee, Robert E. 94, 96, 101, 102, 105, 150
Lehmann, Herman 40
Linnville raid 55
Lipan Apache 39, 40, 57, 84, 91, 92, 135, 144
Lipan Apache Band of Texas 46
Lipan warrior 42
Little Egypt 107
Lomeria Grande 13, 39
Longstreet, Lieutenant James 82, 87
Los Almagres 35, 63
Los Tejanos Diablos 68
Luckett, Colonel Phillip Nolan 119
Luckett's Third Texas Infantry 117

M

McCord, Colonel James E. 131
McCord's Frontier Regiment 120
McCulloch, Captain Benjamin 55, 68, 74, 112
McDonald, First Sergeant Walter 102, 104
McRae, Lieutenant C.D. 122
Menard 35
metal arrowheads 22, 54, 58
Meusebach-Comanche Treaty 56
Meusebach, John O. 67
Mexicano Presidial 62
Mico Creek 110
Middle Archaic 20
militia 49, 71, 77, 112, 143
Mission San Antonio de Valero 24, 62
Monte del Mesa 14, 16, 27, 98
Monteverde 33
Mopechucope 56
Morfi, Father Juan Agustin de 43
Musketoon, Springfield, Cavalry 86

N

Neighbors, Robert 69
Nichols, James W. 72
Nichols, Roland 104
Ninth Cavalry (Buffalo Soldiers) 135
Nowlin, Dr. James Crispin 130, 147, 149
Nowlin, Walter and Richard 149
Nowlin, Walter S. 152
Nueces Massacre 122
Nuestra Señora de Guadalupe 30
Nuestra Senora de la Candelaria 36
Nuestra Señora de la Purísima Concepción de Acuña Mission 25

O

O'Brian, Captain William G. 131
Ojo de Agua de Guadalupe 22, 31, 40, 44, 63, 103

Ojo de Agua San Pedro 32
Old Comanche Trace 102
Old Spanish Trail 102
Owens, Second Lieutenant Wesley 105, 115

P

Paleo-Indians 18
Palmer, Captain Innis N. 98, 115
Parrilla, Don Diego Ortiz 35
Paseo del Aquila 82
Paterson Colt 74
Paul, Captain James 114
Payaya 25, 30
Pedernales River 34, 67
Penateka Comanche 48, 52, 55, 57, 65
Perdiz point 21
Perry carbine 95
Piedras Negras 91, 92, 93, 136
Pinta Crossing 74
Placido 79
Plum Creek 55
Polly's Chapel 88
Presidio de San Antonio de Béjar 30
Presidio de San Juan Bautista 33
Presidio San Luis de las Amarillas 30, 33, 36
Prison Canyon 117, 126
Prison Canyon Ranch 129
Puerta de Bandera 13, 29, 30, 31, 32, 38, 40
Puerta de Los Elotes 29
Puerta de los Payayas 13, 25, 38
Puerta de Verde 33

Q

Quantrill's Partisan Rangers 117
Quantrill, William 117

R

Real, Caspar 152
Red Ghost 109
reduction of the natives 28
Rees, Captain Alonzo 143
Reeves, Lieutenant Colonel Isaac 127
Remolino 136
Republic of Texas 65, 71
Republic of the Sierra Madre 91
reserve military 143
Rio de Alarcón 37
Rio de Pedernales 37
Río Escondido 92
Río Grande Saltillo 60
Rio San Antonio 62
Rio San Saba 35
Rio Verde 16, 30, 31, 37
Rodríguez, José Policarpo (Poli) 88, 105
Roemer, Ferdinand 56, 69
Rubí, Marqués de 36
Ruiz, José Francisco 40, 52, 62

S

San Antonio de Béxar 29
San Antonio de Béxar (or Béjar) Presidio 29
San Antonio de Padua 30
San Antonio de Valero Mission 25, 29
San Juan Bautista 35
San Juan Capistrano Mission 30

San Lorenzo de la Santa Cruz 27, 36
San Lucas Spring 127
San Pedro Springs 32
San Saba River 31
San Saba Trail 32, 33
Sansom, Captain John W. 72, 77, 147
Santa Anna 63
Santa Cruz de San Sabá Mission 26, 35
Schreiner, Charles A. 145, 150
Schwartz, Stephan 126
Schwethelm, Captain Henry 123, 144
Second Federal Line 82, 83
Second Texas Mounted Rifles 119
Second U.S. Cavalry 83, 94
Second U.S. Cavalry Regiment 83
Second U.S. Dragoons 82, 84, 86
Segovia 33
shingle makers 69
slaves, African American 92, 137, 141
slaves, Indian 27, 58
Smith, Clinton L. 40, 55
Smith, Edmund Kirby 94
south fork of the Guadalupe 50
Spanish Pass 13, 25
Spanish Texas 27, 30, 40, 60
Springfield rifled carbine 95
state guard 143

T

Taylor's Eighth Texas Cavalry Battalion 117
Tedro, Philip 109
Tegener, Fritz 122
Tejanos 28, 61, 89, 171
Tejano society 61
Tejas 29, 45
Tejas Indians 30
Teodora, Mimico (Mico) 110
Terán de los Ríos, Domingo 30
Terán, Felipe de Rábago y 33, 35
Texas Archeological Society 17
Texas Declaration of Independence 64
Texas militia units 45
Texas Mounted Riflemen 130
Texas prehistory 17
Texas Ranger Frontier Forces 146
Texas Rangers 56, 66, 68, 71, 91, 114, 131
Texas readmitted to the Union 142
Texas Revolution 65
Texas State Troops 131
Texas Third Infantry Regiment 119
Texas Volunteer Guards 143
Third Frontier District 132
Third Regiment Texas Infantry 118
Thirty-fifth U.S. Infantry 140
Thirty-second Texas Cavalry 128
Thirty-sixth Texas Cavalry 120
Thirty-third Texas Cavalry 123
Thomas, George H. 94
Tonkawa 25, 44, 46
trade rendezvous 45
Treaty of Guadalupe Hidalgo 81
Treaty of Medicine Lodge Creek 57
Treue der Union 123
Turner, Frederick Jackson 15, 153
Turtle Creek 50, 83, 105
Twiggs, General David Emanuel 112

U

Unionists 77, 112, 128
Union Loyal League 77, 122
Urrutia, Captain José de 31

Urrutia, Captain Toribio de 31
Urrutia, Thoribio 44

V

Valle de Verde 16
Van Camp, Cornelius 98
Van Dorn, Colonel Earl 94
Verde Creek 12
Vidaurri, General Santiago 91

W

Waite, Colonel Carlos A. 113
Walker Dragoon model Colt 75
Walker, Sam 73
Wallace, Captain William Big Foot 72, 78
Waltrip, James P. 121
war atrocity 117, 121, 122, 124
war with Mexico 67, 81
Wayne, Major H.C. 98, 107
Whiting and Smith expedition 88
Williams community store 102, 150
Williams, R.H. 110
women, Indian 31, 55
women, pioneer 16, 39, 135
women, POW 128
Woods, Colonel Peter C. 120

Z

Zanzenberg 69
Zaragoza 136

About the Author

Joseph Luther is a sixth-generation Texan who lives in Kerrville, Texas. He earned his doctorate at Texas A&M University and is a professor emeritus of the University of Nebraska–Lincoln, where he taught for twenty-three years, serving as associate dean of the College of Architecture. He also taught for ten years at Eastern Washington University. An enthusiastic avocational archaeologist and historian, Dr. Luther is a member of the Hill Country Archeological Association and is their web master (http://www.hcarcheology.org). He is also an active member of the Texas State Historical Association, the Texas Archeological Society, the South Texas Archeological Association and the Historical Archeology Association. Dr. Luther is a correspondent to the *Kerrville Daily Times* and has written a number of articles about local history.